BORN OF NOTHING

From White Trash and Lintheads to Purpose Across Generations

JASON PIKE
Lt. Col. Jason G. Pike, USA,
Retired

DONALD WILLIAMS, Ed.D.
Educator, Research Analyst,
Retired

ISBN Paperback: 979-8-9889610-4-8
ISBN Electronic: 979-8-9889610-5-5

Library of Congress Control Number: 2026907694

Publishing Consultant: PRESStinely - PRESStinely.com

Portions of this book are works of nonfiction. Certain names and identifying characteristics have been changed.

Printed in the Spartanburg, South Carolina, United States of America.

Lt. Col. Jason G. Pike, USA, Retired
JasonPike.org

Donald Williams, Ed.D. / Educator, Research Analyst, Retired
IamDonaldWilliams.com

Reader Disclaimer: Some photographs in this book are from personal archives. Due to their age and original condition, certain images may appear at lower resolution in print than modern photography standards would allow.

TABLE OF CONTENTS

Acknowledgments v

Prelude vii

Introduction 1

Of Runtish Forefathers 13

White Trash 37

Wage Slavery 49

A Linthead Made Good 59

Slick Legging 77

A Problem of Degeneracy 87

The Germ of Laziness 99

Bloody Thursday 113

White Trash to Trailer Trash 129

The Winding Road 137

Rich Man`s War, Poor Man`s Fight 171

A Note to the Reader 179

Meet The Authors 181

Appendix 185

ACKNOWLEDGMENTS

We would like to begin by thanking our families—those who came before us and those who stand beside us today. The hard years and the good ones, the seasons of want and the seasons of provision, shaped us more deeply than we understood at the time. We carry the strength, the stories, and even the unfinished lessons of those who raised us.

To our parents and grandparents who labored in cotton mills and small towns across the South, your work — often unseen and rarely celebrated—gave us more than a living. It gave us endurance. It gave us perspective. It gave us the opportunity to choose differently.

To our immediate family members, thank you for your patience, encouragement, and grace. Your steady presence reminds us that success is never an individual achievement, but a shared journey.

We are deeply grateful to Peter Baxter, whose research, editorial guidance, and steady hand helped shape this manuscript into its final form. His careful attention to detail, historical insight, and commitment to preserving authentic voice strengthened this book in ways readers may never fully see.

We are also thankful for the friends, teachers, mentors, and brothers who challenged us, corrected us, and sharpened us along the way. As Scripture reminds us, "iron sharpens iron," and we have been shaped by that sharpening.

This book is an attempt to honor the winding road behind us. Any wisdom found in these pages is the result of many lives intersecting with ours. Any shortcomings in its telling are ours alone.

PRELUDE

This book is Born of Nothing: From White Trash and Lintheads to Purpose Across Generations. It is written by me, Lieutenant Colonel Jason Pike, U,S, Army, Retired, with assistance from co-author Donald Williams, and with writing and research assistance from Peter Baxter.

Reader advisory: *Before we begin I want to give you a word of caution. This book contains raw stories, told in the voices of people who lived them. You will come across offensive language, harsh descriptions and painful truths. Some of the words and topics may make you uncomfortable, but I have chosen to leave them as they were spoken. To change the language would be to change the people who told these stories, and that would not be honest. These are not easy stories, but they are real, they reflect the struggle, the poverty and the resilience of people who lived on the margins of Southern life. I invite you to read with that understanding, that what follows is not polished or softened, but truthful, unfiltered and true to the voices of those that lived it.*

I wrote this book in search of my father's origins—born from the forgotten classes of the South: white trash, rednecks, and lintheads. In doing so, I peeled back the layers of a culture shaped by deep, generational white poverty.

This isn't the kind of poverty people talk about in polite society. It's the kind that gets laughed at, dismissed, or blamed on bad choices. But what I found was more than ignorance or addiction—it was survival, pride, and a stubborn kind of strength. White poverty in the South doesn't get the attention or levels of sympathy or safety net that is taken for granted in decent society. It's hidden behind Confederate flags, broken-down trucks, and drawled-out shame. But it's real. And it shaped not only my father—it shaped me.

I hope this book shows you more than just a story. I hope it gives you a raw, unfiltered glimpse into a world most would rather ignore.

Lt. Col. Jason G. Pike, USA, Retired

INTRODUCTION

There ought to be hunting parties that got up to chase them down,
and exterminate `em, just as we do rats.
Harriet Beecher Stowe

SOMETIMES, WHEN I WAS A KID, my daddy would collect my brother and me from school, and on our way home, we would detour through the backroads around Fingerville and Lake Bowen. While he'd be driving around, with a beer between his knees and a cigarette between his fingers, his mood would grow melancholic and reflective. Sometimes we would visit the old Fingerville textile mill, a big, boarded-up red brick building on the North Pacolet River, and there we would drive among the abandoned old row houses where the mill-villagers and lintheads once lived. At other times, we'd creep up on a trailer settlement on each side of a dirt road, off the street, where a community of poor white folk lived. We'd call it the Shack Town. There he'd park up discreetly, and we'd sit quietly as he smoked cigarettes and took it all in. Sometimes he'd reflect on his own life, on poverty—what it's like, what it means, and how it degrades the body and the spirit.

"Hey Jake," he would say, "there's no good side to poverty. It's all bad."

He did that from time to time, I guess, to remind himself, and to remind us, where he came from. He told us that seeing it all made him want to work harder, to build that wall thicker and higher. Nevertheless, despite living in fear of it, of ever having to go back to it, he never moved very far away from it.

A school portrait of Jason Pike in first grade. That year, he failed English and was held back, forced to repeat the grade. Reading and understanding written instructions never came easily, and the struggle followed him through school. Yet, what began as a weakness became part of his story of grit—proof that setbacks in childhood did not define his future. Through perseverance, Jason went on to earn advanced degrees, serve his country, and publish his own work, turning an early obstacle into a lifelong testimony of resilience.

MY NAME IS JASON PIKE, AND I AM a retired military officer from South Carolina. A few years ago, I wrote a memoir of my thirty-one years in the U.S. Military, and it was only then that I began to seriously investigate the details of my father's background and origins. Although it had always been understood that his childhood was deprived, I never quite appreciated its extent until then. By then, he was dead, and so was my mother, and it was too late to talk to him, or hear those stories again. The only person still alive who had known him as a child was old Fred Pike, and by then, he was elderly, and living in deep retirement. I figured, before he followed the old folk to the grave, I'd better track him down and get some of those stories down on paper.

Years earlier, when I was a young kid, I did indeed collect recordings of many of those stories, and it is one of my deepest regrets that I never kept those recordings. I had a beat-up old Sony cassette player, and when the two of them got together, I'd sneak up and sit close by and listen, covertly recording their conversations. As the beer cans stacked up and the whisky bottle dwindled, and as the room filled with smoke, their tales would grow more lurid and profane. I grew to love those stories, and then, as I grew older, I began to appreciate that revival of the old Southern storytelling tradition that ran in their veins. Somehow, that collection of cassettes has been lost, and gone with it the tales and reminiscences of two men who were icons of their culture and generation.

Fred and Daddy were cousins, or maybe second cousins—no one really knows for sure. Family relations in some parts of the South are difficult to trace. Everyone was related to everyone else, and asking one of the old folks who was who, and who was related to whom, would get them scratching their chins and saying something like, "Well now, I ain't rightly sure, but what I heard one time is…"

The story that I mostly heard was that their granddaddies, William and James Pike, were twin brothers, both of them textile workers, or lintheads, and both of them long gone by the time I came into the world. My great-granddaddy on my daddy's side was James Pike, known as Jimbo, and as the story told about him, and his brother Will, is that their people were sharecroppers from around the Inman–Spartanburg,

SC, area, who lost their land during the Civil War, and ended up as sandhillers. Sometimes working, but mostly moving from place to place.[1]

There were a lot of folks in that same situation. They used to say it was a rich man's war and a poor man's fight, and that surely was true. When the plantation system came down, and the slaves were freed, the old system of working the land using gang labor fell away. Large landowners got to parceling out their holdings and leasing blocks to tenant farmers, who in turn often used sharecroppers. Black men and women, who had once been slaves, were released onto a landscape that was not friendly to them, where they had no cash reserves, no savings, no banks, no lawyers, no doctors, and surely no representatives. They worked as sharecroppers and sometimes as laborers. Those who were poor before the Civil War were outright destitute by the end of it. The campaign was mostly fought on Southern soil, and they say when two bulls fight, it's the grass that gets trampled.

After that came the railroad and the carpetbaggers, and those who had fought the war and lost everything because of it were left to wander through the wreckage in ever-deepening destitution. Among those carpetbaggers were the northern textile barons, looking to exploit the natural resources and dirt-cheap labor of the South. It was also the peak of the Industrial Revolution, which introduced factory labor to the South. What they offered was low-skilled, labor-intensive work, and as those red brick monuments, those cathedrals of industry, rose across the countryside, poor whites found refuge in employment. Fred Pike, like many others, was born and raised on the Inman Mill Hill, and so were his mama and daddy before him.

---

[1] 'Sandhillers' was a term used in the 19th and early 20th centuries to describe poor, rural white people—especially small farmers or squatters—living in the sandy, infertile regions of the American South, such as the Sandhills of North and South Carolina, parts of Georgia, Alabama, and Florida, and some areas of Arkansas and Texas.

Jason stands beside the towering remains of a four-story cotton mill, pointing to the bricked-over window bays that once let in natural light. In the early days of mill work, windows were left open for ventilation—but managers soon noticed that workers were drawn to the view, slowing production. To maintain discipline and output, many mill owners had the windows sealed, prioritizing efficiency over comfort. The result was a darker, hotter, more controlled environment—one of many sacrifices made on the altar of industrial progress."

Fred and my daddy met for the first time at Inman High School in about 1945, when both of them were in the ninth grade. Fred was living with his parents in the mill village, while my daddy was living in Inman with Cora Pike, who we all figured was his step-grandmother, even though she was younger than his mother. Cora married old Jimbo, my great-granddaddy, when she was thirteen, to help him take care of a bunch of his kids from an earlier union. My grandmother, Frances Pike, was one of those kids. No one knows what happened to Jimbo's first wife, or even if he was ever married before, just that he had a small tribe of children from somewhere.

"Ol' Jimbo, well he'd lay down with anyone, and might near anything!" Fred laughed, in his uniquely profane way. "Prob'ly they all had different mothers, maybe. Couple of them maybe was mothers and sisters."

As I said, one of those sisters was Frances, my grandmother, who was known later in life as Margie, and she was said to be about ten years older than her stepmother. They say that Cora and old Jimbo were also related, and the way things were in those days, they probably were. They were part of a sprawling, interrelated community strung out between the mill towns of Spartanburg and York counties, and across the state line into Henderson County, NC. My daddy lived for a time in Hendersonville, NC, squatting in a shack settlement on the side of Stoney Mountain.

Stoney Mountain is a name that I heard much when I was growing up. It's a granite-crusted, heavily wooded outcrop rising out of the metro area of Hendersonville, NC, and in whatever story I heard about my father's early life, that name was always a big part of it.

"Lotta poor folk lived thereabouts," Fred reflected. "Lotta white trash living up there on that mountain, just living in shacks and lean-tos on squatted county land. Moonshiners, what today would be drug dealers, I guess, and they was low living, scavenging folk, lotta them living just like animals up there, coming down sometimes, robbing and stealing, living on trash. Diff'rent type of folks."

"Were you white trash?" I asked him.

He reflected thoughtfully for a while, replying at length.

"People maybe would say that… when we was growing up. That we'd be white trash, prob'ly, is what they would likely say. But we was workin'—white trash, those people on the mountain, wouldn't get stable, just move all over the stinkin' place. They'd move all the time, just white trash. folk need to settle down, need to get a home."

"Was my dad white trash?" I inquired, cautiously.

Fred's eyes narrowed further.

"He'd whip your ass if he ever heard you say that out loud. But yeah, your daddy's people was white trash, for sure. Ever'one in the South was poor in them days, but white trash was somethin' different. Somethin' about those folks living up on the mountain that's just different."

Fred could usually be found at home, in a recliner, surrounded by books, ready at an instant to plunge into an argument, a debate, or an intellectual brawl. He was a fighting man, and his eyes sparkled with that driving curiosity that never faded, that passionate, aggressive intellectual fervor that I remember so well. Although his days of fist-fighting were over, he was still outspoken, argumentative, and uncompromising. I used to think to myself that he was part Einstein and part Archie Bunker. As a philosophy major, he was a deep thinker, widely read, well-traveled, and broadly experienced, but beneath all of it, well he was just still a linthead.

"We was poor," he reflected, "dagummit we was poor, but we was not white trash."

To him, that was an important detail, as it was—and still is—in so many places, to a lot of people.

"White trash live up there on the mountain," he said again. "Livin' in a dirt-floor shack, shittin' out back, and use mountain laurel leaves to clean their asses. They don't care. Your daddy's daddy—he was really his stepdaddy—was ol' Nick Wright, one-legged Nick Wright. No one knew who your real granddaddy was. Your daddy was a bastard child. Ol' Nick, he'd search through the trash cans and dumpsters at night and he'd come home with food and rags, and, you know, that's how they lived. I remember one time your daddy told me they took him to the hospital to have tree bark pulled out of his ass. He was eatin' tree bark and resin 'cause he was damned near starving, he was eatin' that crap as food. What makes a boy do that—start eatin' pine resin, and maybe dirt? He was starving. That's white trash right there, no mistaking."

"Anyone lower than white trash?" I asked.

"In the old days?" He reflected, rasping his chin with yellowed fingernails. "Only blacks. Today? No one lower than white trash."

My daddy was born on February 25, 1934, in Inman, SC. As the story goes, Frances Pike and his daddy were working as agricultural labor at some place outside of town, and the midwife, an elderly black woman, was paid a bucket of corn for the delivery. Both his birth certificate and his obituary comment only that he was the son of Frances Wright. No one rightly knows who his natural father was, and nor, really, any details of his relationship with his mother. It was the time of the Depression, and down in the South, men came and went with the seasonal demand for labor. Either way, after my daddy was born, his father carried on along his way, never to be seen or heard from again. At least, that's what they say. When my Daddy drank, he would often call himself a bastard child. Someone, I cannot remember who, told me they had heard from someone, who read it somewhere, that his daddy was killed in a knife fight in a hobo camp somewhere in Texas. Maybe that was true. It seems like it might have been.

"No one knows," said Fred, when I asked him. "No one even knows his name. They say your daddy's mama was a prostitute. Prob'ly was, thinking about it, and I guess that was how your daddy was conceived. Single girl in the 1930s, still in her teens, all alone caring for an illegitimate baby boy—prob'ly would have been a prostitute, at least part-time. I recall that she was a tomboy, kinda mannish—these days prob'ly she'd be a lesbian, prob'ly was in those days too. Your daddy told me one time he saw her in bed with a woman. Women pay for it too, they say, 'specially in them days. Frances was tiny, no titties, but she was pretty, sure was."

After the birth, and the filing of the birth certificate in Inman, Frances Pike drifted for a decade or so through the border counties of North and South Carolina. That went on until, eventually, when my daddy was about ten or eleven, she settled down with an older man—a ne'er-do-well, one-legged drifter by the name of Nick Wright. She moved in with him and lived for the remainder of his life in a lean-to shack on the side of Stoney Mountain, above what was then the small mill town of Hendersonville, NC.

Jason at mill, highlighting the smokestack. In the past, these cotton mill smokestacks were emblems of pride for the mill communities, symbolizing industrial progress and economic stability. Standing tall as iconic landmarks, they often rose 100 to 200 feet, releasing plumes of smoke that signified bustling activity and the production of textiles that fueled the local economy. Constructed from brick or concrete, these structures were engineering marvels of their time, designed to vent the steam and smoke from coal-fired boilers that powered the mills. Many communities even named streets or neighborhoods after the mills, reflecting the central role these smokestacks played in daily life and cultural identity.

Nick Wright is another obscure family member, known better through stories than any real, documented history. They say around there that crimes cannot be solved because no dental records exist and the DNA is all identical. There may be some truth to that, but either way, it is in the nature of white trash that babies are often born, live, and die completely outside of the system. Records do show that he served in the Marine Corps in Europe during WWI, and, as the story goes, lost his leg in 1918 during the Battle of Belleau Wood. There is another story, though, told to me by my father, that Old Nick Wright served behind the lines, and lost his leg under a train in Montgomery, Alabama, while he was a hobo. Either way, the picture that I can piece together from the patchwork of family anecdotes and recollections is one of a depressed, broken-down man living, like so many others at that time, on the far fringes of decent society. He offered sanctuary to a desperate and itinerant woman who was also lost in the ruins of the post-Depression South. He took her in, along with her surly, suspicious, and life-scarred bastard child, who, even at the age that he was, was well accustomed to taking care of himself.

These days, a narrow, black-top road winds up the side of Stoney Mountain, with new and newish houses built on steep lots to maximize views of both the city below and the blue hills of the Piedmont in the distance. Here and there can still be found the shacks and derelict houses where the white trash once lived, and a few places where they still do. Sometime in the 1970s, my dad and I drove up that road, when it was still a dirt track, and there, on a wooded lot on the north slope, with a tiny creek running behind it, stood the collapsed ruins of that old wooden shack.

A breathtaking view of the rolling Blue Appalachian Mountains stretches endlessly into the horizon. Early settlers were drawn to this remote wilderness by the promise of land and freedom—escaping governments, rigid class systems, and the burdens of society. But isolation came at a cost. Generations grew up without access to formal education, healthcare, or opportunity. Over time, poverty deepened, crime emerged, and genetic isolation led to inbreeding in some pockets. A distinct and often misunderstood class of people emerged— proud, resourceful, yet unfairly labeled by outsiders with the derogatory term 'white trash.'

We stepped out of the car and walked around. To me, it looked like a pile of firewood left out in an overgrown grove, surrounded by mountain woodland. My daddy looked into the ruins and saw that the floor was still just dirt. He shook his head, and said, mostly to himself, how hard it must've been to raise a family in a place like that. The shack had been built out of scrap wood and shingles, comprising a single room and a tiny porticoed porch. There was no evidence of plumbing or wiring, and no hint of an outhouse or any other type of convenience.

The ruin was probably about fifty years old, and it would only be a couple of years before the mountainside was parceled up and that old structure burned or hauled away to the dump. I have been able to unearth no record of when Nick Wright took up residence in that shack, or who owned the land, nor under what terms he lived there. In all likelihood, as was the case in a lot of places, the land was squatted. In the late twenties and thirties, there were shack towns all along the river, and up along its creeks and tributaries. There was a large shack settlement on the wasteland surrounding the Berkley cotton mills, where the only work at that time was to be found. Probably, in those days, Stoney Mountain was just the same.

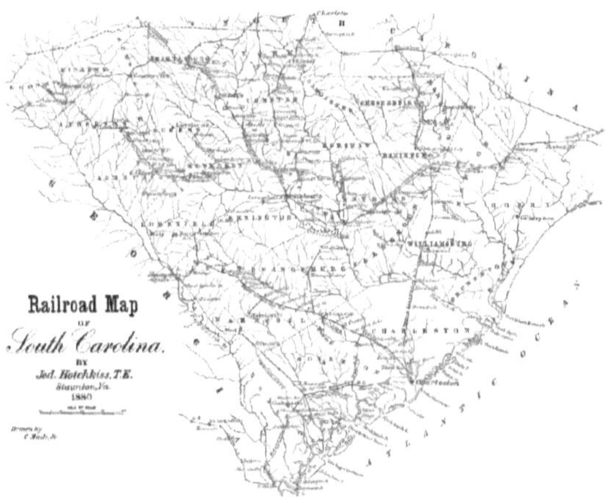

Railroad map of South Carolina, a region central to the rise of the Southern textile industry. Cotton mills required four key elements to thrive: access to transportation, water, power, and a steady labor force. This area provided all four. Rivers powered machinery, railroads moved raw cotton and finished goods, and the local population—often displaced farmers and sharecroppers—supplied the labor. These conditions laid the groundwork for the mill towns and communities that would shape the economic and social fabric of the Carolinas for generations.

Nick Wright took up no formal employment, and as my daddy told it, he mostly scavenged in the town at night, coming back sometimes with scraps of food and clothing from the trash cans, and probably stealing where he could. Even within that marginalized community, his disability struck him lower than most, and my daddy would sometimes tell of them fetching water in a pail from the creek, taking a dump out back, and using those mountain laurel leaves to clean up their asses. One thing I knew for sure was that they cleaned their asses with mountain laurel. Old Fred never forgot that detail.

"Cleaned their asses with that ol' mountain laurel," he would say. "That's what your daddy always told me. Leaves of three, he said, let them be—'cause them be poisonous."

Frances did what she did, meanwhile, and probably there were a lot of women thereabouts doing just the same, and in quick succession, there followed four children. One day, my father, the bastard child, tired of being picked on by his embittered, destitute, and broken-spirited stepfather, left. As the story goes, the two got into it one day, as they often did, but this time my daddy picked up a chair and broke it over ol' Nick's head. Whenever my daddy told that story, he would smile to himself. With just the clothes he was wearing, he would say, he walked out of the shack and down the mountain. He was thirteen years old, and he never went back.

Of Runtish Forefathers

We inherit more than land and blood;
we inherit the things our people cannot say
Anonymous

THIS IS WHERE THE PAST AND PRESENT MEET. Here I introduce you to my family, some you can still find on Stoney Mountain, near Hendersonville, NC, and others who live only through the stories that have been handed down. What you will find in this section is a mix, the voices of my 'Runtish Forefathers', men and women of small stature and hard living, who survived against the odds in the Appalachian hills, and alongside them the stories of my living relatives, still carrying forward the same spirit, the same grit, and in some cases, the same struggles. This chapter is about more than genealogy. It is about how memory and story keep people alive, how the laughter around the present day kitchen table can echo voices from generations ago. It`s about understanding where my people came from, and about how their lives on Stoney Mountain still shape who we are today. So, as you read, imagine two timelines unfolding at once: the family I know and walk with now and the ancestors whose stories rise out of the red clay soils of the Carolinas. Together they form a tale of two cultures, and the forefathers who left their mark on me.

A timeworn shack rests quietly beneath a tangle of overgrowth, its sagging porch and scattered remnants whispering of a bygone era. Scenes like this once dotted the Southern landscape less than a century ago—humble homes that bore witness to hard work, resilience, and "simpler times."

MY MOM WOULD OFTEN SAY, in moments of anger or frustration, that I was "not quite right." I was kept back to repeat first grade, and tested thoroughly, with results that came back a lot less than optimistic. I displayed some diagnostic symptoms of a learning disability, and my parents were advised to be realistic about my academic future. Throughout my school career, I was encouraged by teachers and school counsellors to forget my often-stated ambition to attend a college or university, and to content myself instead with a trade, at best, or the military.

Then, when I was about eight or nine, I injured my knee in a swimming pool accident and ended up with a bad case of osteomyelitis. The effect of it on my life currently is pretty minimal, but at the time, I was left with a limp, which only added to an overall sense of physical and intellectual frailty. I developed what folks called "Pike's monkey walk," a shambling, discoordinated gait that reinforced the feeling many people had that something was just not quite right with that Pike boy.

Although it bothered me none, it caused both my parents a whole heap of worry, considering some of the poor examples of humanity that populated my father's side of the family. My mother expressed it sometimes, sensing that some of those darker traits of inbreeding and mental and physical deficiency had surfaced in her youngest son, and although my dad did not so directly say it, I am pretty sure that he worried about the same thing.

I FLEW TO ATLANTA IN THE FALL OF 2024, collecting Peter, my research assistant, in Greenville, before heading to Hendersonville to check into the local Marriott.

Peter, just for the sake of context, was at the time my research assistant, an educated Englishman of South African origin, who was about to embark on a cultural journey like no other. He helped me in some of the research aspects of my memoir, and I recall his response then to meeting some of my father's side of the family for the first time. He said: "I had no idea that people in America lived this way." Well, they surely do, and he was about to see and experience a whole lot more.

The objective of the trip was to try and burrow more deeply under the skin of that side of my family. Our first stop was Aunt Rita's house. I had her address, and we drove up Stoney Mountain Road a few times, passing the pin on my navigation app a few times before we went in. The darn place looked so clean and well-tended that I thought we must surely have the wrong address. As we entered the driveway, crunching over recently laid gravel, an elderly woman stepped out of a set of open French doors and onto the porch. This was Aunt Rita.

She was a handsome, silver-haired woman in her late seventies, dressed in a crisply laundered green satin jumpsuit. In her hand, she held a looped length of green oxygen line that led back into the house and was attached to a nasal cannula under her nose. She greeted me with a stiff hug, shook Peter by the hand, and invited us in.

Aunt Rita was the eldest of the four children born to Frances and Nick up in that old shack on Stoney Mountain. She had a sense of what I was there for, and she made it clear from the get-go that she had nothing to say about much of anything. I had made mention in my memoir of some of the nature of my father's childhood, and made a few observations on the character and circumstances of his family. Aunt Rita was the only one I am aware of who read the book, and I can be pretty sure that a few of those descriptions upset her.

"Jason," she began, as she arranged herself on a sofa in a cluttered but clean and ordered room. "I haven't seen you since you were a teenager."

"Could have been," I replied.

"Had to be," she said, with a smile, nervously winding that oxygen line between her fingers.

For a moment, she sat, regarding me with a sweet, engaged smile. I looked around. I have never visited Aunt Rita at her home that I could remember, and the surroundings were definitely not what I expected. The house was on two levels, and in conversation, she told me that her son Lonnie lived on the lower level. He was a tarot card reader who worked from home and gave comfort to her in her old age. The living room opened through a set of sliding glass doors into a large dining room, with an archway that I guessed led to the kitchen, the bathroom, and the bedroom. The floor was covered by an old, seventies-style shag pile carpet that had recently been shampooed and vacuumed. It seemed to me that she had gone to a lot of effort to clean the place up for my visit. I guess she had a point to make. Whatever I might find anywhere else, she at least did not live the way I described it in my book. She was not white trash. She was a proper and decent person who lived in a real house, and she was going to make sure I left understanding that fact.

"Jo-lyn called me," she said. "She told me you would be coming."

"Well, I…" I began, but she interrupted me sharply.

"Jo-lyn won't say nuthin', and I won't say nuthin' neither."

"I understand," I said. "I ain't here to cause any trouble."

"Jo-lyn lives right down the road," she went on. "Go down the road here… turn left outside my house, and then take a right…"

"How long has Aunt Jo-lyn lived there?"

She paused and relaxed a little.

"Well, fifty-five years now, I expect. It was Mama's house after Daddy died in 1970."

"That was Nick Wright? The one with the peg leg, right?"

She smarted, as if from the lick of a whip, and looked nervously down at her hands.

"Well, we called it a wooden leg, 'cause he got it from the VA. He was in the Marines, he lost his leg fighting in Europe."

"He lost his leg in the military?" I asked, in feigned surprise. "I heard he lost it under a train, that he was a hobo."

"That was a lie," she replied sharply, her eyes flashing. "That's what was told before, and that's what turned us against your daddy. Him and my daddy just didn't get along, is all, so he went to live with Cora, and that was Mama's stepmother."

"He and my dad got into a fight, and…"

"I have no idea," she cut in, firmly. "Mama never told it, and we don't talk about that. Your daddy and my daddy, they just didn't get along. That's all I know."

"Is that 'cause he was the bastard child?"

"I reckon so."

"They got into it one day, and Daddy broke a chair over Nick's head, and walked down the mountain, never went back?"

"Well, I don't know," she said. "Mama never spoke it, but that's kinda what I heard. All I know is they didn't get on. It was before I was born. All I know is your daddy left and went to live with Cora in Inman, with Betty and Louise…"

"Betty and Louise," I replied, latching on to what could be a fruitful angle. "I remember them. Betty was kinda strange, as I remember."

"That she was." She smiled.

"My dad told me that she was probably born of incest."

"Wouldn't surprise me." Her eyebrows arched, with a sage and knowing nod of the head. "Wouldn't surprise me."

It didn't bother her so bad hearing such things about Betty and Louise.

"If they was, who would it have been?"

"Well," she reflected, perhaps feeling on safer ground. "If it was incest, that means somebody in the family was related, and that means it was likely Jimbo. Must a been ol' Jimbo, 'cause he was their daddy. He married Cora when she was just thirteen, and Betty come outa Cora, so—maybe they was related somehow, or maybe it goes back further. I reckon it was him, though. I reckon, I don't know. Nobody else I can think of. They might have told that story just because she was a little squirrelly, but, you know, a lot a folk do incest in these parts—you know, in the South. They got an old saying down here, 'If it ain't good enough for your own family, then it ain't good enough for me.'" She chuckled. "I don't know. Lotta crazy people, them Pikes. But I don't really want to talk about it, Jason. I don't want to say nothin' 'gainst nobody."

This photo depicts Jim Pike, Jason's great-grandfather. Though Jason never had the chance to meet him, Jim left behind a large family tree so complex that even he might have struggled to explain it. He spent most of his life working as a sharecropper, enduring the hardships of rural Southern life. At just 14 years old, Cora Pike became his wife, beginning a long, difficult journey together that shaped the generations to follow.

"One time," I went on. "I can recall, my daddy got everyone in the family together, the Pikes and the Wrights, and whosoever, and tried to figure it out who was who, who was related to who and how it all fitted together."

"I remember that!" she said, laughing. "I was there, I went down with Aunt Elsie and Aunt Dutch."

"Well, he couldn't figure it out, so he handed the list to me and told me you figure it out Jason!" I laughed. "Well, hell, I couldn't figure it out. Don't think anyone could, probably."

"Well, you ain't gonna figure out nothin' now, 'cause they're all dead and buried."

A thoughtful pause followed, as we both reflected on that fact. Yes indeed, they were all dead and buried, and that was that.

"So where was Nick Wright born?" I asked.

"Right here in Henderson County."

"My dad did show me the place where they lived on Stoney Mountain. It was just a shack on the side of a hill, with a dirt floor…"

She did not care for that, and her eyes flashed again.

"But why are you so interested? Because I don't think about it Jason? That was then, and I'm getting too old to reminisce about that."

"Fred Pike and my daddy went up to Stoney Mountain and looked at that shack…"

She raised her hand to stop me. Her smile strained as she fretfully curled the plastic oxygen tube between her fingers.

"You see," she said nervously, a look of sincere anxiety in her eyes. "I never seen it. I never did see it, and really, I don't want to talk about that, and Jo-lyn won't talk to you no how. She told me you was coming up today, and she said it ain't nobody's business what happened. A lot of it is lies that go back for years. Jo-lyn won't say nothing. Mama didn't talk about stuff. We weren't supposed to talk about nothing. That's just the way it was. We weren't supposed to know nuthin', and we didn't know nuthin'. It's just how it was."

This absolute refusal to yarn, and tell stories about childhood, home life and family was, to my mind, a sure sign that Aunt Rita had abuse in her past. Southern folk love to tell stories, and a happy childhood would be filled with such stories. When the family closes ranks, it is almost always because they are hiding something, or protecting someone.

I tried a different approach.

"My daddy was born in Inman in 1934. He was delivered by a midwife, a black woman, who was paid a bucket of corn for the delivery."

She laughed.

"I remember her. She delivered Betty and Louise, and I think she delivered your memaw, too. She delivered a lot of the babies born in the town in those days."

"My dad was the oldest," I said. "Then number three was…?"

"Nick," she replied. "He went into the Navy for four years, and he met a girl and married her."

"And number four would be…?"

"Jo-lyn, and then Vic."

"Any more that we know of?"

She laughed. "Well, your guess is as good as mine."

"Who was my father's father?" I asked.

She stiffened. "Now that's what I don't want to talk about," she said. "Mama never said nuthin' and I got nuthin' to say about it neither. She never mentioned it, and that was just the way it was."

I stuck at it.

"Only, Daddy was thirteen when he and Nick got into it, and he told it to me that he only lived there on Stoney Mountain with Nick and his Mama for a few years, and then he left, went from family to family before Cora took him in. What happened for those ten years that went before?"

"Well, Mama and Cora never really got along neither. Cora, even though she was ten years younger, was Mama's step-mama. I guess Mama had her ways, she done some things, in those Depression days, you know, times was real hard, and Mama was, well…"

I did not say it, but I thought it. That might have been a step too far. My father's mother was a prostitute, wandering the county with a bastard child. It was not for that reason that her daddy would not take her in. They say that every second child among the white trash is illegitimate. It was the question about how she was, in bed and such, that was a blight on the name of the family. She was a lesbian, as old Fred remembered. The word in the family was that Bobbie, Aunt Rita's son, living down there in the basement, was homosexual. Lonnie McLane, Aunt Rita's nephew, and Aunt Jo-lyn's oldest son, told me about it one time.

"I just can't stand that shit!" he said to me. "That boy is a faggot. He's as queer as a eight-dollar bill. Mama won't have him in the house."

That maybe explained some of the estrangement between the two sisters, and it also was why Frances could not take her bastard child home, moving instead from hobo camp to sharecroppers' shack, taking up with different men, prostituting, and sometimes taking up with women. Word of that sort of thing gets around, and her people would have known—that she was a prostitute, and a lesbian.

"What did she do in those days, when Daddy was a little kid?"

Aunt Rita looked down at her hands, twirling that green oxygen line between her fingers, and for a long time, she was quiet, her eyes moist and her lips pursed.

"I ain't gonna say nuthin' about that," she replied at length. "And Jo-lyn ain't gonna say nuthin' neither. Mama told us to say nuthin', and nuthin' is all that I'm gonna say."

I said to Peter as we left:

"That's how it is when there has been abuse in the family, maybe sexual, surely physical. The family closes in, and no one says a damn thing. It gets to be a habit. Mama warns the kids to say nothing, and they know that if Daddy get sent away, times are going to be a whole lot harder. That is why it is so often in the family, because it's safer that way."

ALTHOUGH AUNT JO-LYN AND UNCLE CARL lived just a few blocks away, their's was a completely different world. The family home was, and still is, a three-bedroomed house wedged between a small creek and Somerset Drive. In recent years, the neighborhood has begun to gentrify, and so the house has grown pretty noticeable for its dereliction. How it came to be in the family is one of those persistent mysteries that seem to cloud the entire, enigmatic history of the Pike clan. From what I have been able to figure out, Frances rented the place in the early 1970s, after Nick Wright's death, maybe after picking up some army money, or maybe a military life insurance. After renting for a few years, it was purchased, and the family has lived and grown in it ever since. Now it appears that it belongs to Aunt Jo-lyn, who has, in my lifetime at least, been the family matriarch.

The drive from Aunt Rita's house took just a few seconds, and as I stood outside in the cool twilight of a Carolina evening, I reflected on the many times, throughout my childhood, that I had visited this property. In all of that time, I had not once seen it painted, or cleaned, or repaired in any way, and it was just as I remembered it. A few more window panes were missing, and now boarded up, and the door, once white, was stained brown with the scratch marks of generations of dogs. I recall one time my daddy gave Aunt Jo-lyn money to have the shingles replaced, but the work was never done. I'm pretty sure there were a million other priorities besides the roof, and the same broken shingles were still on it, except now with a blue tarpaulin draped over the whole thing.

I was reminded of a story. One of the extended family had a daughter one time who had a brain tumor. Funds were raised in the community for medical care, but instead, the daddy took the money and bought a used car. That's just how a lot of these folk are. The community raised money and donated, but typical of white trash, in some weird alternative reality, you can bet they will always waste it on something dumb and stupid.

I walked up to the front door, Peter walking behind me, picking his way through the trash, looking around him in amazement. I knocked, and the door was opened almost immediately by a heavy-set, tawny-haired woman dressed in an oversized t-shirt and a pair of leopard print pajama bottoms. I had seen her before, on a previous visit, but I could not, in the moment, remember her name, or what her relationship to the family was. She regarded me with a face jaundiced and emotionless, her black eyes deep-set and ringed with dark shadows. As an ex-military medical officer, I could see immediately that she was suffering from chronic anemia. I introduced myself, and she acknowledged me without expression, holding the door wider to allow me in.

Inside, I was met by an intense and familiar smell, a combination of dog and cat urine mixed with the concentrated odor of stale cigarette smoke, pot, and compacted human habitation. It brought back a flood of memories. The front room was as I remembered it, almost unchanged in the fifty years or so of my recurrent visits. The young woman rearranged herself on an old and soiled sofa, wrapping a blanket around her shoulders, and returning her attention to a tube television in a broken cabinet against one wall.

A long-haired and bearded youth in his early twenties was also on the sofa, also wearing a pair of pajamas, this time in plaid print. I could see at a glance that he had a club foot. He briefly acknowledged us before returning his attention to the screen. A little boy of four or five sat between them, also pale, and clearly also iron-deficient, breathing in the cigarette smoke that hung in the air. The room was cluttered with trash and filth, a bicycle, an old cast-iron stove, and piles of clothing and cardboard boxes.

Besides the television, the room was unlit, although a bright light shone in through an open door to the kitchen. The silhouette of Uncle Carl appeared, framed by the doorway, and when he saw me, he cackled.

"It's Jason!" he cried.

He reached out, and I shook his hand; his two contracted fingers pressed against my palm.

"Jo-lyn," he called. "Jo-lyn, it's Jason."

A door opened to my left, and there stood Aunt Jo-lyn, the same short, anxious-looking woman I had known since childhood. She stepped out into the living room and reached up to hug me. The woman on the sofa remained with her eyes fixed on the television, almost as if she was living in some parallel, unrelated world. It reminded me of some of the family compounds I visited in the Philippines and Thailand, where a lot of people lived in small spaces, and lived their lives separately, but in the same space. People come and go all the time, such that the notion of individual space or privacy becomes meaningless.

Peter and I were led into the kitchen by Aunt Jo-lyn and offered a seat. Peter's job was to film and record the encounter, and mine to coax as many yarns and stories out of the family as I could. He took a seat at the kitchen table, his back to the wall, and his eyes wide with wonderment at something that he had never seen the likes of before.

He told me later, once again, that he had no idea people in the United States still lived that way.

While there are not very many left, there sure are a few.

The smell in the kitchen was far more pungent than in the living room, cluttered as it was with old furniture, some factory-made, but most piecemeal and jerry-built with nails, screws, and box wood. The faucet over the sink was trickling, and as we were settling in, two mongrel dogs, both ancient, and I would guess incontinent, came in and sniffed around. One squatted and peed in the corner without exciting comment or remark from anyone.

Aunt Jo-lyn was a very ordinary-looking woman, slight, probably in her mid-seventies, blue-eyed, kindly and soft spoken. She was missing most of the fingers on her right hand after they were mangled in a textile machine when she was working as a teenager at the Berkley Textile Mill. I inquired, and she reminded me that currently she worked on the cleaning staff of a retirement home, although lately she only worked three hours a day, just enough to keep up the payments on the house. (Omg!—how old is the mortgage on this place—sounds like a whole other story!)

Carl McLane, her husband of fifty-five years, had probably at one time been pretty conventional in his own world, but now he was kind of a relic of a bygone age. At eighty-seven years old, he was a tall, rake-thin and angular man, talkative, humorous, and cheerful. He still spoke in that quaint, old-timer's Smokey Mountain English, champing his jaw, and laughing happily for the pleasure of an unexpected visit from ol' Jason.

"He's got teeth," Aunt Jo-lyn remarked, with a wry and weary look. "But he won't wear 'em, and he's got hearing aids, but he won't wear 'em neither."

A tall, blond man with a buzz cut swung into the room. He was barefoot, about forty-fiveish, dressed in shorts and a Carolina Panthers t-shirt. This was Stan. Stan, one time, had a reputation as a lady killer, and sure enough, he was a good-looking boy, even with most of his front teeth missing. Peter was introduced, and then Stan and I got to talking about the army.

"You were in for a couple of days?" I said. It was not a question, just to get the subject rolling for the sake of the hidden microphone.

"A couple of months," he replied, looking a little bit sheepish. "I did some basic training, and I coulda done it easy, but it was my kids. Social services contacted the Army while I was at Fort Jackson and told them my kids weren't being properly looked after and they sent me home. The guy told me, he was a major—I think he was a major—that you gotta be in the army or out, he told me. You gotta be army or you ain't. You cain't be worrying about yer kids. So, they sent me home."

Uncle Carl, in the meantime, had gotten to telling a joke. It was a joke about three men who visited a brothel in Gaffney, and the girls they rented were called Mary-Belle, Ginger-Bell, and Liberty-Belle. No one was listening, and he laughed gaily to himself at the punchline, which was something about Liberty-Belle's crack.

Meantime, Stan turned to Peter, and they spoke for a few minutes as another figure shambled in from the living room. This was Lonnie, a giant of a man, six feet three in his bare feet, and north of 395-pounds. We shook hands. Lonnie was the oldest, and my favorite of the boys. He was unscrupulous, violent, and uncouth, and as white trash as they come.

"Show us your tattoo!" I asked him, and with a smile, he turned his back, and lifting his t-shirt, revealed an arched, home-made tattoo across his back that read: "Redneck."

"You a redneck?" I asked him.

"Damn straight!" he replied, laughing. "Hillbillies come from the hills and redneck come from the swamp! I come from the swamp. Damn straight I'm a redneck!"

Lonnie was a brute. A hard-looking man, running to fat in middle age, but limber, agile. He had a crushing handshake, despite his fist mangled from years of untreated breakages. There was about him an air of latent violence, as if that friendly exterior could turn on a dime. He had served several stretches of prison time over the years, mostly, as he said, for good stuff—fighting, guns, and drugs. "No perverted stuff!" he would laugh, as if perverted stuff was a pretty regular thing in those parts, and it probably was, and still is.

I told him what we were doing in town, and what we wanted, and then I asked him:

"If you're a redneck, what's the difference between redneck, white trash and hillbilly?"

He arched his eyebrows and thought about that for a while, leaning against a cabinet, wearing a pair of green Crocs, camouflage-pattern pajama bottoms, and a red t-shirt. He was spooning out a bowl of ice cream.

"Not much, really," he replied. "They all white trash, really."

Just then, Miss Patty, Lonnie's girlfriend, came into the kitchen, and taking a seat, she joined the conversation.

"Redneck is a Georgia cotton picker," she said. "Before the Civil War, redneck was literally a cotton picker, then they was drafted during the civil war. They got their necks burned by the sun, picking cotton. That's where the name come from."

"So what is the definition of a hillbilly?" I asked.

"Jed Clampett," Stan interjected, and Miss Patty laughed gaily.

"Yes, sir!" she said. "Jed Clampett, damn straight, that's a hillbilly right there."

Miss Patty was wearing a hoodie, so it was difficult to guess how old she was, but she had hard times written all over her face. At one time, she might have been pretty, but she was surely no longer, and she, too, was wearing Crocs on her feet and red, plaid-pattern pajama bottoms. When she laughed, her chest rattled, and her voice was graveled from the chain smoking.

But she was also bright and engaging, and like everyone else in the room, she introduced herself to Peter and chatted to him for a while about this or that. They all accepted him without question, and showed sincere curiosity in the fact that he was British and had lived in South

Africa. It meant nothing to them, of course; none of them had ever been out of the country, probably not even out of the South, but they were kindly folk, and the house was home to a lot of people.

"Hillbillies is just country boys," Stan went on. "Bluegrass music, clogging and flatfoot dancing, and all that sorta stuff."

"Mama's people," Lonnie added, for emphasis. Then: "Not so much nowadays—well, we hillbillies still, I guess—my grandma—I never met my grandpa, but what I hear about them, they was hillbillies. They lived up on the side of the mountain. Hillbillies live up on the mountain, you know what I mean? They had kids to work the fields, they grew everything they had. They go huntin' and fishin', they work on the farm. They just farmers is what it is, pretty much what hillbillies is, they grow their own food and raise their own hogs. That's how they made it. I guess they sold some of their stuff maybe. Some of them are millionaires now, because of what they do—selling meth and fentanyl and stuff, and killing and curing their own meat. A lot of them still live on the land so they don't raise no suspicion. They just don't look it, 'cause they don't want to account fer that money, but some of them got a whole lot of money."

"So what's white trash?" Peter asked.

"Redneck!" Lonnie replied, with a chuckle. "Same thing."

He scraped up the last of the ice cream from his bowl and set it in the sink.

"They used to call white trash crackers," I said. "You ever heard of that?"

"Oh yeah?" he replied.

Miss Patty, still listening with sincere interest, added.

"Crackers what niggers call white trash, its niggers that call rednecks white trash, that's exactly where that come from."

"Rednecks," Lonnie went on. "They run around and get their ass in trouble, they don't give a damn, they don't like authority, they get drunk and show their asses. They're always the assholes in the crowd, is what it boils down to. When we was growing up the rednecks all watched NASCAR racing and had Bush Hog hats."

He laughed, and Patti laughed too. Stan had left, and Aunt Jo-lyn was somewhere else in the house, and Uncle Carl, all the while, was rambling on about a trip he made to Arkansas when he was a lineman in the 1970s, and was ignored by everyone.

I turned to him.

"You a redneck Uncle Carl?"

"What?"

He leaned forward, smiling.

"A redneck! Are you a redneck?"

"What's that?"

He put his hand to his ear.

"A redneck!" shouted Miss Patty. "Is you a redneck?"

"A redneck?"

He smiled sweetly, his blue eyes twinkling behind his spectacles.

"Sure, I'm a redneck. I sure am."

"Are you a hillbilly?" I asked.

"A what?"

"A hillbilly!" came a chorus of amused yells.

"A hillbilly? Hell no! I ain't no hillbilly. I'm a darn redneck, is what I am. A redneck."

He laughed. Everyone laughed.

"You proud of being a redneck?"

"Damn right!"

There was a pause. Uncle Carl sat back in his chair and appeared to ponder the question in his quiet world.

"Rednecks drink," Lonnie went on, meantime. "Rednecks don't do drugs. I guess if you want to know the difference between rednecks and white trash, then it's rednecks and country boys who drink and get rowdy, but it's the white trash that do drugs, and sell drugs, live in a mess, don't work. Used to be moonshine, but now it's meth and fentanyl and stuff. We rednecks—I ain't saying we don't do drugs—but we ain't white trash."

"White trash what killed Martin Luther King," Uncle Carl interjected abruptly, rousing himself. "Martin Luther King Jr., killed by James Earl Ray, that was white trash, Jason. That's white trash right there."

He fell silent again, staring reflectively at the floor.

Pretty soon, the intel was leaked that I had a bottle of bourbon in the trunk of the car, and with that, they all pulled up their chairs around the table. The liquor was poured into a single glass tumbler for Ralph, and mugs and coffee cups for the rest of us.

"To this day," Uncle Carl proclaimed, following up, I guess, on the same theme. "I have more damned black friends than I have white. I don't have a damned thing against the blacks. Matter of fact, years ago, I had a friend, Marvin McGee, big ol' rough country boy—well, I had a black friend too, and his name was Silas. Well Silas called by one day, and we were sitting around this very table, and Marvin come walking in—now I don't go with the word 'nigger', the Lord put everyone here, white, black, and it make no difference to me if it make no difference to Him—well Marvin come walking in, and when he get to the door right there, he looks at Silas, and he says 'who's yer nigger friend Carl?'"

Uncle Carl rose in his chair, and glared at me intently, his jaw champing, and his eyes blazing.

"I stood up!" he went on. "…and I said, I said, I don't have no nigger friend! I said I got a black friend, and his name Silas, but I don't have no nigger friend! And I said, don't come by my house again with the word 'nigger'."

"Well, out the door he went, and I ain't seen him since. That's white trash Jason, that's white trash right there boy. The Lord brought 'em here, and who am I to turn 'em away. When I'm dead and gone, I'll be going to Heaven or Hell. I hope it's Heaven, but if I go to Hell, it ain't gonna be for cussing no black person."

Lonnie, meantime, was scrolling on his phone, listening to his father, smiling from time to time as a familiar story was retold. As we were leaving, Lonnie followed us out and asked to borrow a few bucks. I gave him a twenty and told him I'd pay him to show me around. We agreed to meet for breakfast the next morning. The next morning he called and told me that he had been high all night on some stuff and would call after a couple of hours sleep. He did not, but he did call the next morning.

"SO HOW MANY TIMES YOU BEEN ARRESTED?" I asked him.

"Hell, thirty-three, thirty-four times," he replied, laughing. "All the money I spent on fines I coulda bought me a house, but like I said, all of it good stuff. Drinking, drugs, and guns. No perverted stuff. Nuthin' like that."

LONNIE CLIMBED INTO THE FRONT PASSENGER seat of the rental and we took off up the road. At six foot, three inches, and definitely north of 395 pounds, it was a squeeze.

"Gonna educate you boys today huh?" he said.

"Yeah, you gonna have to educate us," I laughed. "Especially Peter."

I handed Lonnie a one-hundred-dollar bill.

"Get you some more later," I said.

"What for?" he asked.

"Oh we're just gonna talk some crap."

"Okay buddy," he replied, tucking the bill into his breast pocket.

"Are you pretty good at talking crap?" I asked.

He laughed.

"Yeah, I done that once or twice."

We drove on for a while.

"So tell me about that damn weapon of mass destruction thing?" I began, and he arched his eyebrows the way that he always did, and laughed.

"Oh lord," he said. "You goin' in right to the good stuff."

"I heard you got taken in for shooting a weapon of mass destruction. What the hell was that about?"

He chuckled.

"Mama and Daddy left town to go to Gatlinburg for their twenty-fifth wedding anniversary, so me and my buddy Dusty Farmer decided we was gonna have a party. Before we went down to the bars we got drunk. We'd have to get drunk before we went anywhere, because me and Dusty, we couldn't afford to get drunk at the bar because we couldn't afford the prices of it.

"We were drunk by the time we got there, pretty much, or at least half way, and then when we got there, we got real tore up, and we just started trouble. We was loud, you know what I'm saying, and people, they mostly don't like it when you get loud, especially if you been drinking. Someone told us to settle down and stop being so loud, that's when the mess started. The doorman he didn't like that, and one thing led to another, and we ended up fighting with the doorman. He hit Dusty with one of them swing out baton sticks. I hit him from behind with some darn thing, split his head wide open, and whenever he come to, he ain't gonna be hittin' no-one else with that darn thing!"

He laughed a big phlegmy, rattling laugh.

"Back home," he went on. "Smoking crack and drinking, we got into it with the neighbor. I had an SKS, some piece of Chinese crap, seven-point-six-two, and Daddy filed the darn pin down. He don't admit it to this day, but he did, he did somethin'—fooled with a few things or whatever, to make it fully automatic. And we were shooting out the back door, just messin' around with it—we wasn't bothering nobody, just chillin' on a Friday night. Had two thirty-round clips taped together like Rambo… it had a bump stock on it, a bayonet and everything—put it out the back door and brrrrrrr! Just like that. Let go a full clip.

"By then, we were into a gallon of liquor and maybe five hundred bucks worth of rock. Man, we was high, you know what I mean? We was on the moon, son! We was hanging out with Elvis. I was shooting out the slide glass door because I thought the shells would fly back in the house so if—when, not if—the law arrive, there won't be no spent shells lying out on the deck where they can find them, you know what I mean.

"Anyway, I went out the first time, and brrrrrr… about ten minutes later, when I did it again, I only got about two rounds out and the red and blue lights come on, and the cops, dogs and guns come outa everywhere, dude. They had the whole house surrounded. They thought I was shooting at them. All the city and some of the county was there.

"I started fighting with them, and they put the handcuffs on. They didn't just put 'em on, the boys slapped 'em on, slapped dude, and it hurt like a sonofabitch. It was somethin'. I was charged with all kinds a stuff, all kinds a damn stuff, though mainly for discharging a weapon of mass destruction, 'cause it was full auto. With all the fines, and lawyers and stuff I paid for, I could've bought a brand new house. Mama and Daddy are still paying the house payment right now. They had their house paid for before that."

"Yeah," I said. "I thought they would have had their house paid for by now?"

"They did," he said. "It's my fault that they don't. They refinanced the house to get me outa jail and to pay lawyers and court fines. They didn't have to. I didn't know it was gonna happen until they had already done it. Because of that, everything was downgraded to a misdemeanor, 'cept kickin' the police dog. I kicked the darn police dog, and they sure didn't like that. That was a class C felony right there."

We began our drive up Stoney Mountain Road, along a winding thoroughfare that made its way through a patchwork of gentrified neighborhoods, dominated by new homes on lush properties. From time to time, Lonnie pointed out a derelict single-wide or a sprawling shack complex where a few of the old families lived.

"Don't drive too slow," he would say, anxiously, obscuring his face with his arm. "I don't want them to see me out here taking pictures of their house. If they see me, and they see you—a cue ball head like you—they think I'm bringing the law to them. Could go badly for me. End up dead in a ditch, you know what I mean."

"WHAT DO YOU KNOW ABOUT YOUR GRANDADDY?" I asked him.

"Not much. Grandma and Grandpa died before I was born, and they don't talk too much about it. I hear it was bad though, the way those folks lived in them days, the way your daddy lived. It was messed up. I ain't surprised your daddy left. They say he knocked the daylights outa old Nick Wright, my grandaddy, when they got into it one day, and he left and went down to live with Cora in Inman."

As we drove alongside a sprawling property, he narrowed his eyes and rasped his chin.

"I wanna say Daddy told me this was where the shack was, where they lived. Nothin' there now, it's all gone—goddamn Jason, don't drive so slow!"

I sped up and rounded the corner on a familiar setting. Yes indeed, where now an extensive, shingle-sided home stood, was where my daddy and I picked through the ruins of that lean-to shack. There, Frances Pike found a home with her ten-year-old, illegitimate son. Her fate was then intertwined with the consumptive, morally depleted Nick Wright, one leg missing just below the knee, and his days and nights tortured by the agonies of a crippled old soldier.

Old Nick Wright and my dad did not get along. The first ten years of my dad's life were itinerant. My guess is that his father shipped out pretty soon after the birth, probably following along the labor migrations of the Depression era, leaving Frances to drift from shack-town to shack-town, a part-time prostitute, mostly. Maybe she got pregnant by Nick, and maybe not, but either way, she became his wife mostly because he asked. He was some bit older than her, and already a pretty derelict and broken down old man. Maybe he picked up some Army money, but the stories tell of real deep poverty. Even in a time when Southern cities were ringed by shack-towns, the story of Nick and Frances Wright is miserable.

"You ever talk much to Aunt Rita?" I asked, and he shook his head.

"Not much," he said. "She's kinda stuck up, she don't like to mix too much with us. She married good, so she thinks 'cause she got money that she better. We all come from the same damn place, she and us—'sides, that boy of her's, Bobbie, he a faggot, and no-one likes that."

"She talk much about the old times?"

He shook his head.

"None of them talk about the old times. Don't none of them say nothin' 'bout that stuff at all, you know what I mean."

"Musta been pretty bad."

"Musta, I guess."

We drove on past the ambulance service buildings that at one time had been Balfour Elementary. Every day my daddy walked down the side of the mountain, just by his own reckoning, no one told him to do it, and attended that school. They say he just showed up one day, no birth certificate or nothing, and told them he wanted to go to school. He lived in that shack, an illegitimate child, his step-father an onery, embittered old bastard, and the two clashed frequently. Through the nomadic years, he had learned to stand up for his mother and himself, and even as a boy, he was more than a match for old Nick.

"You ever hear the story of my dad breaking a chair over old Nick Wright's head?"

Lonnie laughed.

"Damn right. It runs in the family. Didn't just use a chair neither. Gave his stepdaddy a beating they say. Thirteen-year-old boy beatin' up on a grown man. Your daddy was a hard man, they tell me. I used to love it when your daddy came to visit. He always brought a whole bunch a stuff, and everybody got something, and everybody got slipped a few bucks. I remember I used to think I was the only one, and that I was special, until I figured out that all the kids got the same."

He laughed, and I laughed, because that was sure true. My daddy left that shack, and left that life, and with an overwhelming determination to never return, he made good.

We drove on in silence.

"Do you work?" I asked him after a while.

"I don't work," he admitted. "But I make mine. Mama and Daddy don't question me, and I got nothing to lie about, she knows all my choices, and she don't ask me no questions. If I got money, they don't ask me where I got it. It's not always what they think it is, but you know.

"You know what I'm saying? I'm not a thug. I don't go round robbing people, you know what I'm saying? I don't go round stores stealing stuff, I just swing. It's just dope—pills and pot—or I collect for someone, or somethin'—sometimes I just take care of people's business for them, depending on the situation, somebody don't pay what they owe, or whatever. I be careful though, don't want to get my ass whipped, although it does happen, it happen quite a bit actually. I've had my ass whipped more than I done the whippin'."

We drove on for a while in silence, until at length he remarked:

"You wanna visit some of Nick Wright's family, it'll shock the daylights outa you?"

"Damn right!" I replied.

"Alright, you asked for it. Pick me up same time tomorrow, only I ain't riskin' my ass for two hundred dollars. If I'm gonna walk into some place where I might get shot at, I need to be numb enough to not care when it happens."

I waited.

"Three hundred!" he said, casting me a sideways glance. "And bring me three big bottles of Wild Turkey 101. Not the regular stuff. The 101. If I'm gonna do this, I need to be damn near bulletproof on the inside."

I smiled to myself.

"Sure thing boss! We're heading out of town for a few days to catch up with an old buddy in Rock Hill, but we'll be back."

"Well, give me half of that three hundred now!"

WHITE TRASH

WHITE TRASH, REDNECKS, HILLBILLIES, there are a ton of names used throughout recent history to describe much the same thing, and there are more: cracker, lubber, dirt-eater, sand-hiller…the list goes on.

Old Fred Pike knew his way around American history, and from his sagging bookcase, he pulled out a few old volumes.

"This one here." He said, "is *Georgia Scenes*, by Augustus Longstreet. He was the one who created that famous character of Ransey Sniffle."

Just for the sake of context, *Georgia Scenes* was published in 1835, and was one of the first folkloric depictions of life in the new American colonies. Ransy Sniffle was kind of a Brer Rabbit type character, applicable to many different scenarios that described a particular type of individual common on the fringes of respectable society. This is how Ransy Sniffle was described by Longstreet:

> Now there happened to reside in the county just alluded to a little fellow by the name of Ransy Sniffle: a sprout of Richmond, who, in his earlier years, fed copiously upon red clay and blackberries. This diet had given to Ransy a complexion that a corpse would have disdained to own, and an abdominal rotundity that was quite unprepossessing. Long spells of the fever and ague, too, in Ransy's youth, had conspired with clay and blackberries to throw him quite out of the order of nature. His shoulders were fleshless and elevated; his head large and flat; his neck slim and translucent; and his arms, hands, fingers, and feet were lengthened out of all proportion to the rest of his frame. His joints were large and his limbs small; and as for flesh, he could not, with propriety, be said to have any. Those parts which nature usually supplies with the most of this article--the calves of the legs, for example, presented in him the appearance of so many well-drawn blisters. His height was just five feet nothing; and his average weight in blackberry season, ninety-five.[2]

Ransy Sniffle was the stereotypical cracker, sandhiller, dirt-eater, and, of course, white trash. He was the first popularized character, a kind of early Jethro Clampett, or Bo and Luke Duke, appearing wherever a tale needed to be told about white trash. He resided in many places, and under many

---

[2] Longstreet, Augustus Baldwin. *Georgia Scenes* (Upper Saddle River, N.J., Literature House, 1969) p54

sets of circumstances, but always anti-social, always belligerent, always looking like death warmed-up, and always on the take.

Ransy Sniffle also represented the natural progression of an immigrant population sent out to the colonies as the 'waste people' of the British Isles, the old country's 'spleen and liver', draining the '…ill humours of the body.'[3]

That was probably true, and it is difficult to argue against the certainty that the dregs of European society surely did make their way to the Americas, either as bonded labor, fugitives, or transported convicts. Either way, a good many of them found themselves unable to survive in a free condition in what revealed itself to be just another feudal society. Marginalized and bonded, little more than slaves, they made use of what was easily available to them, and that was the wilderness, and the endless space beyond. Space was something absent in the old country, where land was something sectioned off and owned by the lords and the aristocracy, and so many of the lubbers and crackers and sandhiller simply took to that wilderness. There, through the generations, they became feral, creating a caste that many saw at the time, and many continued to believe, was just *different*.

As old Fred Pike told me many times, everyone in the South is poor, but white trash is something *different*.

What is *different?* What does *'different'* mean?

"Well." Said Fred. "They say it's cultural, and maybe it is. Maybe all those generations living out there on the fringes created a different species. Who can say? Maybe it's true. There surely were a lot of people who figured it then, and a lot that still do. White trash is just different."

The presence of extreme white poverty in the South has been so widely observed and noted, and there has been so much written about it, that the phenomenon must have been widespread and very visible at one time. As I got to digging into it, I read through a lot of

---

[3] A sermon upon the eighth verse of the first chapter of the Acts of the Apostles: Preached to the Honourable Company of the Virginian Plantation, 13. November. 1622. By John Donne Deane of Saint Paul's, London. Reference is made to the American colonies as the spleen and liver of the old country.

commentaries and memoirs written about the antebellum South, and many a contemporary took note of it, commented on it, and usually had an opinion about it.

From left: Jeff McLean in a blue shirt, his father Ralph McLean in the center, and the author, Jason Pike, on the right. The photo captures not just faces, but the continuity of family, friendship, and the ties that bind across generations.

During the colonial era, 'lubber' was the term most commonly used to describe a particular class of person living beyond the margins of colonial administration. Mostly, they were people who had escaped either from bonded servitude, slavery, or the law, and because it lay beyond the rule and government of the English Crown, they opted for the wilderness. Sometimes they confederated with native American groups, forming organized and armed communities, and these had a reputation for menacing and intimidating the colonists from just beyond their reach.

According to Fred, the term 'lubber' was first coined in 1728 by William Byrd II, a member of the landed aristocracy who undertook the task of surveying a disputed boundary between Virginia and North Carolina. Occasionally, as he toured the frontier, he would stumble on pockets of these isolated and regressive people, and his descriptions of them just ooze contempt and loathing. They were mostly European, but there were some fugitive black slaves among them, and numbers of native American women. They were not, Byrd noted many times, compatible with civilized society, and for sure they were not. They were degenerate, licentious, and unscrupulous. What's more, they were violent, cunning, sideways-glancing, and rarely to be trusted. I recall Fred chuckling when he told me that story.

"Ain't much has changed." He said.

Although William Byrd, and many others, commented on the clear moral degeneracy of these people, he and his survey crew were happy to fraternize. Lubber women, although probably not the most beautiful, were nonetheless available, compliant, and creative, and sexual adventure among them was without risk, except, of course, for the almost certain eventuality of a dose of syphilis. On the whole, lubber women were mixed-race, and their social position concurred with the traditions of the native people. Lubber women were, for that reason, regarded as the primary beasts of burden of their communities. Typically, the men among the lubbers were quite content to delegate all labor to them, and themselves to just languish in the idleness, squalor, filth, and ill-health within which they all lived. They were white, that much worked in their favor, but in every other respect, they behaved like maroons or native tribes, and, in fact, they were often in alliance with both.

That was an early manifestation of white trash, when the colonies were closed in by Indian country, and the southwestern taper of the Appalachian uplands. As the life of the colonies progressed, however, and the dynamic of land ownership was established, things began to change. The wilderness became less accessible, treaties were established with the Cherokee, and the British aristocracy reconstituted itself as the dominant landowning class. From the fertile lowlands of the South, the vast estates of the new planter class emerged, with armies of black slaves working the land. Cotton was cultivated on a massive scale, and out of the virgin landscape arose those classical revival mansions that so defined that particular moment in history. White labor was unnecessary and socially stigmatizing, so most poor whites took to the sandhills, and the barren margins of the fall line.

Then, because, at the time, land was the only real vehicle for upward social mobility, those without legitimate access to it began to push more aggressively into the trans-Appalachia frontier. Eventually, the term 'lubber' fell into disuse, and was replaced by 'cracker', which maybe described more accurately a class removed by geography and economics from the mainstream of colonial life.

Crackers were different from lubbers because they tended to be more proactive, clannish, and aggressive. They behaved, not like the Ransy Sniffles of the South, those lethargic, half-dead 'lubbers', the landless victims of a feudal society, but almost as a culture of white maroons actively carving out their fiefdoms within the isolated mountain hollers and the sandhills of the fall line.[4] When captured and presented before the law, they displayed lip-curling contempt for authority, and a fearless disregard for the conventions of civilization. They had the British authorities of the time scratching their heads and wondering what could be done with them. They were described by the colonial authorities as '…a lawless set of rascals on the frontiers of Virginia, Maryland, the Carolinas and Georgia.'[5]

Perhaps more worrying to the British colonial authorities than the criminality and degenerate moral standards of these crackers was the potential threat they posed to the colonial structure of law and governance. While the term 'lubber' implied idleness, filth, squalor and moral degeneracy, the term 'cracker' was much more emblematic of active criminality and an antisocial culture that threatened, not only the securitym of the colonial social order but also the well-being of the colonists themselves. That was a very different state of affairs from that created by the mostly apathetic lubbers, and much more challenging to the colonial administration. It is probably also worth noting that the 'lubber' class still existed, and was still to be found wandering listlessly on the fringes of orthodox community, but they did not excite quite the same revulsion and terror as the violent and unpredictable crackers.

---

[4] *Maroons* was a name given to communities of escaped slaves founded in remote and inaccessible places, or beyond the colonial boundaries.
[5] From a letter dated June 27, 1766, from Colonial official Gavin Cochrane to the Earl of Dartmouth

So disruptive along the frontier were these communities of crackers that a vigilante movement was born, known as the *Regulators*. For a brief period, in the fall of 1773, the Regulators wrought havoc along the frontier, as they violently attacked and destroyed cracker settlements, which, in the end, proved just as disturbing to the colonial authorities as the crackers themselves. The victims of this local vigilantism were not always crackers, but also 'sandhillers', or impoverished, and somewhat productive small-time planters who had settled the bleak, infertile sandhills of North Carolina.

This brief period marked, if not the end, then certainly the beginning of the end of the cracker phenomenon. By then, in any case, the Revolutionary War was in full effect, and at the end of it, new terms came into common use, most notably 'dirt-eaters', and maybe most enduringly, 'poor white trash'.

A glimpse into the rugged character of the Carolina mountain families, reflected in both their look and way of life. The photo shows not only kinship but also the weight of circumstances that have shaped each of them in different ways.

IT IS DIFFICULT TO IMAGINE THESE DAYS, in an era of unprecedented prosperity, that such a vast area of the Southern landscape, in the antebellum era, was characterized by the grinding poverty of so many marginalized whites. It was during the antebellum era that the idea solidified of those poor and degenerate whites living on the fringes of the plantation economy being somehow a different, deviant subculture of the white race. Probably the best-known writer of that era—in the century between the Revolutionary War and the Civil War—was Harriet Beecher-Stowe, famous for the romanticized portrayal of the slave South in her book *Uncle Tom's Cabin*. Besides that, she wrote several commentaries that breathe life into some of the raw historical data supporting the extent of poverty in the South. She devoted an entire chapter of her book, *A Key to Uncle Tom's Cabin*, to the emerging classification of 'poor white trash.'

What I found interesting about this piece is how distasteful these people were to the mainstream of society, and how completely hopeless their situation seemed to that emerging culture of enlightenment and philanthropy. Although Harriet Beecher-Stowe probably represents the essence of that developing social consciousness, she, too, looked down on the lowly cracker with a sense that there really was no hope of redemption for those wretched people. This was the dawn of the abolition movement, both in the Northern states and in Europe, and while the abolitionists lamented the moral degradation imposed on enslaved blacks by the system, Harriet Beecher Stowe was part of a chorus increasingly laying the blame for white poverty at the feet of that very peculiar institution. She writes: *But it will appear that the institution of slavery has produced not only heathenish, degraded, miserable slaves, but it produces a class of white people who are, by universal admission, more heathenish, degraded, and miserable.*

That is a very bold claim, and one ought to wonder what she means.

She goes on: *...the filling up of all branches of mechanics and agriculture with slave labor necessarily depresses free labor. What branch of* *useful labor opens a way to its (poor white) sons? Would he be a blacksmith ?—The planters around him prefer to buy their blacksmiths in Virginia. Would he be a carpenter?—Each planter in his neighborhood owns one or two now. And so coopers and masons.*

In other words, why hire skills and labor when you can buy them for cheaper? For free labor to compete with slave labor, the freemen had to be willing to work for less than the cost of maintaining a slave. Some plantations did hire free white labor, simply because slave labor was at times scarce, but rates of pay were almost universally sub-economic, and thus they became: "*…the pest of the neighborhood, the scoff and contempt, or pity even of the slaves. The expressive phrase, so common in the mouths of the negroes, of `poor white trash`, says all for this luckless race of beings that can be said.*"

The ambition of these people, Ms. Beecher-Stowe also remarked, was to scrape up enough money to buy a slave or two, and thus elevate their own status by having someone lower than themselves to be contemptuous of. God help, she said, "*…any unfortunate negro man or woman, when an execution or the death of their proprietors throws them into the market, and they are bought by a master and mistress of this class.*"

The story was told at the time of a travelling clergyman who put up for the night in the miserable shingle shack of a family of precisely this class. The family owned two slaves, a husband and wife, who had been oriented in a fine home, taught all of the graces of civilization, and were then sold as part of the clearance of a deceased estate. The two begged the clergyman to buy them, fell on their knees, and prayed to him to relieve them of their circumstances, but he could not. From the gifted pen of Harriet Beecher-Stowe, this story is filled with pathos and hopelessness, and it further illustrates the contempt by which persons of a reasonable standard of civilization regarded "*…the most horrible and ferocious of mobs.*"

Generally, it is understood, and most literature will support this, that the term 'white trash' emerges from the earlier phrase 'poor white trash', or 'po white trash', used by black freemen and slaves to describe the white laboring class. It is probably worth adding that indentured white labor was still not uncommon in the decades and years leading up to the Civil War. Generally, poor whites eschewed any kind of labor, preferring to exist as virtual hunter-gatherers in the countryside rather than submit to a kind of industry that the institution of slavery had degraded and cheapened. Still, blacks and whites of every class used the terms 'poor white trash' and 'crackers' to describe those impoverished whites of very low status.

In the years leading up to, and immediately following the Civil War, concurrent with the emergence of the sciences of sociology and anthropology, more interest began to be shown in the cause and effect of this blight on the beloved notion of white superiority. Clearly, there was a significant number of light-skinned people who were not objectively superior to blacks and Indians, and many who were obviously inferior. By the 1850s, sides were more or less drawn over the slavery issue, and both sides were tempted to use their own arguments to explain the existence and proliferation of white trash. According to the abolitionists, the poor white class had been denied the fundamental right to sell their labor to the highest bidder, arguing that only through accessible education, and free market capital and labor, could this blighted class be uplifted.

Under the principle that a rising tide lifts all ships, both black and white societies would benefit from such a change. Secessionists, on the other hand, argued the Darwinian theory that class delineations were inevitable, even desirable, and that if certain whites had sunk below any acceptable standard of social respectability, they would disappear according to their irrelevance to the principle of natural selection. They had no one but themselves to blame for their situation, and in any case, poor whites were not unique to the South, but were to be found in the northern states as well.

Interestingly, the arrival on the scientific landscape of Darwin's *On the Origin of the Species* revolutionized social thinking, and although historians are quick to point out that Darwin himself did not draw any particular parallels between his theories and those of the eugenicists, by the law of unintended consequences, it prompted a lot of people, including his half-cousin, Frances Galton, to reconsider human populations. Perhaps mankind was not built in the image of God after all. Some began to focus on intervention as an approach to controlling human reproduction, and as a means of manipulating and improving genetic qualities. A lot of people started looking at white trash and figuring that, with a bit of harmless manipulation, they could fix the problem.

Author Jason Pike with Dana McLean, brother of Jeff and son of Ralph McLean. The McLean family represents the deep-rooted connections of Hendersonville—generations bound by place, kinship, and resilience. Moments like this capture not just family ties, but the enduring bonds of small-town Carolina life.

WAGE SLAVERY

They called us lintheads, like we were trash.
But we were proud people.
We worked hard, and we stuck together.
Anonymous

SOMETIMES, ON ONE OF OUR JOURNEYS of reflection, my dad would take me by one or two of the old textile mills that were still operating around Spartanburg and Gafney. By the 1970s, very few of the older concerns were still running. Those great, red-brick structures, their old smoke stacks standing high, were mostly empty and derelict by then, vandalized by local kids, and by the turn of the century, most of them had been pulled down. A few, like the Inman Mill, have been turned into offices, luxury lofts and apartments, but mostly they have all subsided into history.

I recall that we would park up in the parking area as the shifts were changing, at around four o`clock in the afternoon, back a ways so we would not be noticed. From that vantage we watched as people spilled out of the complex, filtered into the parking lot, and climbed into their cars. They all looked pretty broken to me, as if they had been beaten half to death, like the walking dead. I mentioned that to my daddy, and he told me that I may just have learned the greatest lesson of my life. It was the lesson that he had been trying to teach me for a long time. There is no dignity in poverty. It`s just bad, whichever way you slice it.

I do recall that many of the stories exchanged between Fred Pike and my daddy were tales of old Fred`s life as the son of lintheads, who lived their lives, and died, in the Inman Mill Village. The term 'lint-head' is derived from the fact that folks, as they left the mill after their shift, would appear in the community covered from head to foot in fine cotton lint. In the beginning, it was a mildly derogatory term, maybe like white trash, but as the years passed, it became almost a badge of honor, and I recall Fred expressing that sentiment, too.

"Lint-head was working folk." He told me. "My people was poor, damned poor, but they worked hard, and there was never a day that I can recall when there was no food on the table."

Donald Williams, my co-author in this project, also grew up the son of lintheads, in his case, in Rock Hill, SC, where, in the heyday of the cotton industry in the Carolinas, there were quite a number of operating mills.

The Buffalo Cotton Mill, part of the Buffalo Mill Historic District, is located in Buffalo, Union County, South Carolina, along SC Route 215, approximately three miles west of Union City. The mill complex, including the main mill building, mill office, power house, and other structures, was a significant textile manufacturing site built starting in 1900, with its iconic twin seven-story towers constructed in 1901. The surrounding mill village includes various worker residences, a school, and a baseball field/park, all contributing to its listing on the National Register of Historic Places in 1990.

The backstory of the cotton and textile milling industry in South Carolina is probably worth touching on a little bit here, because, while nothing but the ghosts of the old mills remain, it was, at one time, the most visible industry across the Carolinas.

If one were to glance at a topographical map of North and South Carolina, one thing quickly becomes strikingly clear. Along the western boundary of both states, the dominant feature is a plateau region known as the Piedmont, marking the trailing edge of the Appalachian Mountains. A notable characteristic of this landscape is its many fast-flowing creeks and rivers, with names like Saluda, Reedy, Pacolet, Catawba, and many others. With the proximity of large-scale cotton production across the Southern cotton belt, it somewhat stands to reason that a cotton processing industry would begin to develop along this fall line. In the first half of the nineteenth century, the industry amounted to just a few small manufacturers, mainly from the North, who established spinning mills along the water courses around the Spartanburg, Greenville, and Pendleton districts. Markets were mainly local, and the yarn that was produced was pretty crude.

The first of the large, integrated concerns was the Graniteville Manufacturing Company, which began operations in 1849 along Horse Creek in what is today Aiken County. The developer was an individual called William Gregg, who modeled his concept along the same lines as the integrated operations he observed in Lowell, Massachusetts. There, the emphasis was on bulk manufacture, for both local consumption and export, exploiting the technological advances of the industrial revolution, and, most importantly, cheap labor. Gone was the cottage industry supported by the wives of local yeoman farmers and sharecroppers, and in came a system of mechanized manufacture supporting twenty-four-hour a day production that demanded disciplined and compliant shift labor. That labor would be required to live in villages associated with the mill, worship in churches attached to the mill, educate their children in mill schools, and shop in mill stores on mill credit. That is just how it was.

For twenty years or so, the cotton processing industry in the South remained small and low key, until the events of the post-Civil War era began to open up the South to northern investment. Slavery yielded to sharecropping, the railways came, and poor whites from the countryside flocked to the mills, exchanging the uncertainty of sharecropping for the security of labor and a steady wage. The cotton mills, those signature, red-brick monoliths, with their chimney stacks overlooking the countryside, like European churches, came to dominate the landscape, as their capital influence drove local economies. Southern poverty offered mill bosses the immediate advantage of low labor costs, and with lax, and sometimes non-existent labor laws, child labor became a common feature of Southern mill life.

By the 1920s, mill villages, and mill life, were part of the day-to-day existence of at least a sixth of the entire population of white

South Carolinians (until the 1960s, blacks were excluded from the mills), with the company increasingly exerting control over every aspect of life, labor and worship. Some mills were better than others, and a kind of hierarchy developed among mill workers that resulted in an ongoing migration from the lower-paying mills up to the higher-paying establishments that offered brick houses, internal plumbing, electrification, and a range in every kitchen. A style of clannishness developed as the mill villages became more insular and inward-looking, and often the communities that evolved around the villages stood apart from the towns and cities that they were associated with.

A poignant vintage scene unfolds in a textile mill, where young workers diligently operate Saco-Lowell spinning machines, embodying the grueling essence of early 20th-century industrial labor. Both of Donald's grandfathers toiled as child laborers in cotton mills, while many of Jason's family members also found employment in these harsh settings. The air within the mills was thick with cotton fibers, often seeping into the lungs and sparking chronic health issues. Workers, dusted with these fibers—termed lint—upon leaving each day, earned the enduring nickname "lintheads."

I would say that the high point of the mill village culture was probably the first ten or twenty years of the twentieth century, because after that, with the depression and the natural decline of the cotton industry, wages and working conditions began to steeply deteriorate. Although there was a brief uptick during WWII, with an increased demand for cotton products to feed the war effort, the 1950s and 1960s were decades of steady decline. Nowadays, a traveler in the South might still run into an old mill structure, maybe waiting to be demolished, or to be turned into luxury lofts and apartments, but mostly that abundant feature of the Southern landscape is gone. Fred Pike was raised in the mill villages of the 1950s, during the last gasp of Southern mill culture, and his was the last generation to have that experience.

TO GET A BETTER SENSE OF LINTHEAD CULTURE, Peter and I left Hendersonville and drove to York to visit an old college buddy from Clemson who had a story to tell. Donald Williams grew up on the mills hills around Rock Hill and York, surrounded, as he told me often, by forty-four aunts and uncles, and eighty-something first cousins. His upbringing very much echoes that of old Fred Pike, and my daddy in some ways, and like both of those two men, he arrived at the same spiritual crossroads, and he made the same decision. He opted for college and now holds a Bachelor of Science, Master of Science in Agricultural Education, and an Ed.D. in Vocational and Technical Education. Like me, he spent a lot of time in South Korea, and a lot of time in Japan too, so we have a whole lot in common. As college students, we talked about our lives some, but never in much detail, and I thought to myself, this would be a great opportunity to fill in those gaps.

On the way, we stopped in to visit an old army buddy whom I first met at basic training and had kept up with loosely over the years. Like me, he was retired and living up in the hills south of Saluda, a few miles off Interstate 26, and I wanted to show Peter how the real backcountry white trash live. We came off the freeway and followed a state highway for a while before we turned off on a dirt road that wound around a small cluster of wooded hills. There were a few houses on the property on either side of the road, just normal rural homes, clean and well-maintained. I knew that this particular buddy had inherited some small acreage thereabouts, and was living in retirement in a singlewide with a much younger woman, and a couple of her kids. I knew that he was white trash when we met. It is easy to tell, and although I had never visited his property, I had a fair idea of what we were likely going to find.

Barefoot and burdened, young children toil in the cotton fields—an all-too-common scene in the rural South of generations past. Their small frames carry oversized sacks, not just of cotton, but of responsibility. For many tenant farming families, every hand was essential. Donald's maternal grandmother, like countless others, was once discouraged from marrying—not out of tradition, but necessity, as her labor was needed to help the family survive.

Before long, the road narrowed down to twin tracks that seemed like they were hardly ever traveled. You need to be careful in parts like that, coming into homes uninvited. A lot of guns around, a lot of illegal business, and folks do not much care for casual visits. We came around a corner, crowded in on each side by pine forests, and when I spotted the trailer roof above a rise, I stopped and told Peter to wait while I checked to make sure that it was cool. I walked along the track—by then it was pretty much a footpath, with no sign of any vehicle—picking my way over a small field of household trash strewn haphazardly in a semi-circle around the front door of the house. There was no wiring that I could see coming in off the road, and it seemed like the singlewide had been dumped where it was, never leveled, and never hooked up.

I knocked on the front door and, kind of expecting the twin barrels of a shotgun to greet me, I was surprised when the door opened and there was a woman standing on the inside in semi-darkness. The whole scene was like a movie, like a set made up to shoot a scene from *Joe Dirt* or something. She was a short and heavy woman, dressed in a T-shirt and pajama bottoms, barefoot, and with a cigarette between her lips. Her breasts hung low and heavy, and her gut like a sack between her legs. She carried a tallow complexion with heavy, dark rings under her eyes. From inside there seeped a stink that is hard to describe, a combination maybe of cigarette smoke, animal excreta, and concentrated human habitation in an airless and sealed space. Maybe they were growing weed in there, or distilling, or something, I don't know, but it was about as white trash as it gets.

I stated my business, and she looked me up and down before she closed the door. A little while later, my buddy came out—he was as reluctant to invite me in as I was reluctant to go in—so we sat on a couple of upturned buckets outside, in the middle of all the trash, and chatted for a little while. She came out, this time with a soiled baby blue robe over her shoulders, and Crocs on her feet. She sat down on the step and lit a cigarette from a Basic brand pack.

It seemed to me that she might have been an attractive woman in a different world. Her hair was black and her eyes blue, and perhaps if she were two hundred pounds lighter, the impression would have been very different. As it was, if we were looking for an example of a white trash woman to illustrate the type, she was about as good as it gets. I guess she was in her mid-thirties, and he, like me, was in his late fifties, and a couple of times she referred to two kids who, I guess, were in the house. Neither of them was real friendly, and both seemed happy when we left. It was an awkward encounter, filled with suspicion and distrust, but without any sort of sheepishness or self-awareness regarding the utter squalor in which they lived, and I guess they were raising children that way, too.

We drove out of there in silence and got back on the freeway. After a while, Peter said something that again reflected his astonishment that people still live that way in the United States of America. They surely do, and even though they are not many these days, they are still around. In this case, they were probably living on a military pension, with maybe some other government money, and likely he owned the land. So what reason did they have to live that way? Could they not have cleaned up the yard, disposed of the trash in some other way than just throwing it out the front door? Sure, they could, but as everyone told me, white trash is just *different*.

A Linthead Made Good

WE FOUND DONALD WILLIAMS AT HIS HOME IN YORK, SC. He lived, and still lives, on what was the old Carolina Downs Country Club. The course was built by his father-in-law on land bought from a black family who came by it after the Civil War. We headed east on Highway 11, winding through the hills and cotton ghosts of the upstate. Somewhere near the big split with I-85, we passed that giant peach water tower—the one folks either admire or laugh at, depending on which side of the highway they're on. From the back, it looks like a baby's bare ass, and word is, Gaffney's mooning every southbound traveler, and they're proud of it.

And he was pretty proud of the fact that he built his house himself, and a few of the others thereabouts, too. Most of his life was spent as a schoolteacher, finishing out working as a research analyst for the Department of Defense Education Activity, and spending the last fourteen years living overseas in South Korea, then Japan.

He'd put on some weight in the intervening years, but not much, and his hair was beginning to grey. Just like back in the day, though, he was a tall, spare, and angular man, strong featured, and handsome. He spoke with a pronounced regional drawl, clearly heir to the old storytelling traditions of the South, and as we settled into comfortable chairs in the warm glow of a Southern spring, he began his tale.

The story continues in Donald William's voice: My grandparents on my mother's side, Floyd and Viola McDowell, were among those who left the land, and began their married life as mill workers in Gaffney, SC, moving on after a few years to settle in York, SC.

This photograph, taken on Easter Sunday, shows Donald being held by his father while the rest of the family gathers outdoors in their Sunday best. His mother stands to the right, and his three brothers pose proudly in pressed shirts and ties. In Southern tradition, families dressed formally for church regardless of financial standing, making Easter a moment to present one's best appearance, captured here in a timeless family portrait.

LINTHEADS, IN THE WEIGHTS AND BALANCES of class in the Deep South, stood a few points above white trash, mostly for the reason that they worked, held down a job, and led pious, God-fearing lives. Lintheads also stood somewhat higher on the scale than sharecroppers, at least in the immediate postbellum era. The slave era, quite ironically, was one of the major drivers of white poverty—not the marginal condition that defines poverty in the United States today, but the deep, systemic poverty that is really only visible these days in places like India or Africa. The institution of slavery robbed white labor of most access to the market, because large landowners not only owned slaves but also held a monopoly on productive land. Non-landowning whites could not sell their labor, nor could they own land, and it is easy to see where that left them. At one time, white poverty on that extreme level was visible all over the South.

Floyd McDowell, Donald's maternal grandfather, spent his childhood working in the cotton mills, beginning as early as nine years old. Despite the hardships of mill life, he continually sought to better himself. This oil painting stands as a testament to his perseverance and creativity, capturing both his talent and his desire to create beauty beyond the mill walls.

With emancipation came change. The first and most obvious change was emancipation itself, which rendered traditional systems of agriculture—the use of gang labor on large, cultivated blocks of land—mostly obsolete. Although the land itself remained concentrated in the hands of significant landowners, the means of working it shifted from institutionalized slavery to tenant farmers and sharecroppers. This placed cotton production in the hands of small-scale farmers utilizing family members for labor. This was better, in most cases, than sand-hilling and dirt-eating, but not much, and a lot of folk stayed on their sandhills, and kept on eating dirt.

Although there were a few successful tenant farmers working large accumulations of leased land, hiring labor, and getting rich, for most others it was a continuation of the generational struggle. Throughout the Reconstruction era, a majority of Southern workers, white and black, toiled on the land, and it was not until the 1880s, when agriculture began its chronic decline, that people moved away in search of reliable wage labor.

And so it was that, although many in the "New South" may have spent the entirety of their lives on the land, the future of their society no longer lay with the soil, but on the factory floor. Between the beginning of the cotton manufacturing boom of the 1880s and the end of the Progressive Era in 1920, South Carolina became the third-largest textile-producing state in the Union. In 1880, there were about two thousand full-time textile workers in the state, and forty years later, in 1920, there were over forty-eight thousand. They say that in the 1920s, one in every six South Carolinians called a mill hill home.

My grandparents on my mother's side, Floyd and Viola McDowell, were among them, and they began their married life as mill workers in Gaffney, SC, moving on after a few years to settle in York, SC.

Donald (far right) with his three older brothers during the family's annual weeklong vacation. For mill workers, this single week of respite each year was treasured, often spent camping along the Carolina coast. With money tight, families could usually afford only a couple rolls of film— twelve shots to capture an entire year of memories. That scarcity gave each photograph a sense of weight, as if the shutter clicked only for the most important moments. The boys' bare feet, shorts, and sunburned shoulders reveal both the season's heat and the modest simplicity of mill village life. This image, likely taken with a Kodak Instamatic, was among the first color photographs Donald remembers seeing—marking not just a personal memory, but also a cultural shift as working-class Southern families stepped into a new era of affordable photography.

My grandfather McDowell left a charming testimony upon the fiftieth anniversary of his marriage to Viola. It was published as a piece entitled *Life as Theology* in the local church newsletter. The two were married on Christmas Day in 1923, against the earnest pleas of Viola's parents for them to delay, for they needed the help of their last unmarried daughter to manage the land they worked. What follows is a short snippet:

"On Christmas Day in 1923, I was at my house in Gaffney, SC. I wanted to walk uptown about a mile and a half, not knowing that before the day was over, I would be married.

Viola and I had planned to marry, but I had visited her home with her a few days before, and her mother begged us not to marry for a while, saying Viola was needed at home. When I started walking to town on Christmas morning, I thought she was at her parents', but before I had walked a mile, my uncle met me and told me Viola was at his house.

When I saw her, we had not talked but a few words until we were preparing to go to the Probate Judge's house to get married. That was the beginning of fifty years of married life, and as you read this, you will see that there has been joy, sorrow, and disappointment; but as I look back, I love every bit of it."

The couple stayed in Gaffney until 1926, when, with one child, they moved the thirty miles to York. They settled on the Cannon Mill Hill, and my granddaddy took up his employment. They were allocated a two-room house with a light bulb and some form of running water on the porch, and there they settled.

My granddaddy's simple testimony paints a poignant picture of mill life in the 1920s. The church formed the pivot of the community, and a sense of piety, godliness, and simple faith defined their vision of the world. The couple began their life on the mill at a point when the industry was starting its decline. The boom years of WWI, which kept the boilers hissing and the spindles flying, ended when the war ended. Overproduction left stockpiles, and a drop-off in demand created significant pressures throughout the industry. The mill bosses put the squeeze on workers by increasing their machine loads without additional pay. Increased productivity demands put heavy pressure on workers, and I recall stories that both sets of grandparents, and other older relatives, regularly told of twelve-hour days and six-day weeks. It was cheap labor, and the desperation of systemic poverty, that gave the mill bosses the advantage they enjoyed in the Carolinas, and it was something they were not afraid to use.

Mill villagers like my grandparents understood that. Although the mills were tough and poverty a fact of life, it was still better than the land, and a whole lot better than the sandhills. Life went on, folk stuck to it, and survived in the hope and belief that they were building a better life. Then, in 1929, it all came crashing down, and the Great Depression began. Hard times arrived soon after in the southern Piedmont.

"Our first years were very good," my grandfather wrote. "But we had some rough years later as the family grew larger. If Viola had not been a good seamstress and mother, I don't know how we would have fared. A lot of times, she would take hand-me-down clothes and fix them for the children. She always kept them looking fine. I remember it got so rough I could not buy half-soles for the children's shoes and would half-sole them with belt leather straps."

The Depression years, he admitted, were worse still. The revered traditions of the church sometimes had to be missed because of no shoes, no suitable clothes, or sometimes just because there was nothing to tithe, which in those days was truly a moment of desperation.

And still, the mill bosses turned the screws. Workers called the extra machine loads the "stretch-out," and in subtle ways, they tried to resist. There were the militant ones, who sabotaged machines and worked to undermine the company, but most chose, if they were able, to migrate from mill to mill in the hope of finding better conditions. Others supported and joined the emerging labor movement. Under union tutelage, numerous minor strike actions were called—in 1929, for example, twelve thousand workers walked off their jobs—but the cards still remained with the mill bosses, and it was very risky in those days to mount such a direct challenge, and as a consequence, very few did.

Franklin Roosevelt, when he entered office in 1933, offered a lot of inspiration and hope for mill folk who had begun to think of themselves as wage slaves, and many of them, probably most, were. They were promised a "New Deal," and in support of this, Roosevelt signed into law the National Industrial Recovery Act (NIRA).

The celebrations this prompted had more to do with desperate hope than any real promise of change. As far as people could tell, the NIRA guaranteed higher wages, shorter hours, and the right to join a union. The mill bosses, however, saw things differently. Energized by it all, the *United Textile Workers of America*, established in 1901, slipped into high gear, and flying squadrons of militant union organizers and enforcers spread out across the region. Before long, the industry nationwide was in the grip of a general strike, with bands of UTW stalwarts roaming the Carolinas, vowing to shut down every factory in the Palmetto State. If the mill bosses refused to comply, they stood outside the gates and sang until the workers inside joined the picket line. In a few upcountry towns, flying squadrons armed with clubs and bats invaded the plants, trampling foremen on their way to cut off the electricity. No one, they said, was to work as long as the strike was on.

Things came to a head at the Chiquola Manufacturing Company in Honea Path on September 6, 1934. Not everyone supported the strike, and there was intense tension between law enforcement, the National Guard, strikers, and strikebreakers. There were those in my family who were for it, and those who were against it—most were against—and the wider community was split. The mill bosses had no tolerance for union activity of any kind, and they were willing to shut down factories to teach militants a lesson. Usually, it was the families who suffered most. The unions had promised financial and material support for strikers, but often—mostly, in fact—that help never came.

Meantime, after three days of violent encounters and a great deal of shouting, a flying squadron rode into Honea Path, and the shrill of the morning whistle signaled the start of the battle. Those supporting the strike surged forward to block the mill gate, while strikebreakers moved toward the entrance. Clubs and sticks flailed, and then a pistol shot sounded, triggering a ragged fusillade of gunfire. A few minutes later, when the shooting stopped, six strikers lay dead in the dirt and a dozen were wounded. Most had been shot in the back, cut down as they fled. It was a bad day.

Stories of the strike, and of Honea Path, were once embedded in the lore of mill culture. Few today remember those bitter weeks and months, but I recall, even in the 1960s, the stories being told with the same solemn reverence with which people today might speak of the

Vietnam War, or the Twin Towers. The UTW had almost no strike funds, and while a few local churches and charities tried to help, they relied on the mill bosses and local business communities, and so had little interest in supporting an industrial rebellion. Families survived on fatback and cornmeal, and when things got real bad, some began to return to the mills. For many, unions came to be remembered, not as protectors, but as outsiders who made promises they could not keep, stirred up trouble, and then vanished when the hunger set in. That memory of loss, retaliation, and abandonment lingered, and over time hardened into a deep suspicion of organized labor that still runs through much of the South.

Donald and his brothers are pictured with their new bicycles, tricycle, coats, and hats— Christmas gifts made possible through their parents' careful planning. Like many mill families, Donald's parents set aside a portion of each week's wages into a private family savings fund dedicated to Christmas. Though money was scarce, this practice ensured that the children would awaken on Christmas morning to presents under the tree, capturing both the sacrifice of the parents and the joy of childhood in a Southern mill town during the early 1960s.

Most of my family were among the hires and rehires, and the last of them came off the land when Depression conditions destroyed the final shreds of hope among tenant farmers. Many stories from those times were about survival, and the collective determination to rise above poverty. My uncle Robert once told me that my mama, when she was a little girl, wanted to be a missionary to Japan. She must have seen it in a cinema show or something, but she would sit on the porch steps, making up songs in Japanese, even though she could not speak the language at all. In those days, the church was paramount, society was also paramount, and people worked to build and reinforce their community. These people were not wild like white trash; they were trying to better themselves. My granddaddy played the fiddle in a band—he called it an orchestra—and taught himself to play piano and paint landscapes.

Although, in 1939, Roosevelt declared the Depression over, there was grumbling in the mill communities that it might be over for him, but it was not over for them. When war was declared, my granddaddy Floyd, already in his forties, and his oldest son Robert, just seventeen, volunteered to join the Navy. The reason was partly the money, but also a sense of patriotic duty. Both served in the Pacific theatre and returned. At home in York in 1945, they settled back into life in the mill village.

By the 1960s, that old Carolinian mill culture was dying. Labor in the mills was desegregated, and many felt that was the beginning of the end. A few of the larger concerns had already consolidated, and specialized, and the grand red-brick factories that had dominated the counties around Spartanburg, Greenville, and Rock Hill for over a century were beginning, one by one, to fall silent. By mid-century, most mill villages had merged with surrounding communities, and mill houses were either bought by tenants or sold on the open market.

I OPENED MY EYES TO THE WORLD ON APRIL 1, 1959, at the General Hospital in Rock Hill, SC. My mama, Roberta Williams, was sixteen when she married my daddy, and by the time I was born—the last of four boys—she was twenty-one, while my daddy, Lewis Williams, was twenty-four. They both worked for J.P. Stevens Industrial Cotton Mills, Inc., of Rock Hill, SC. My daddy was a "beamer," drawing yarn onto the beam of a loom, and Mama was a weaver.

Among my fondest memories of life in the mill village was Christmas. By the 1960s, conditions were less rigorous than in the early days of mill culture. Mill management would typically throw a Christmas party, with a visiting Santa, toys for all the kids, and other festivities that tied an already close-knit community together. It was also an important gathering for my sprawling family, most of whom assembled at our maternal grandparents' home, where food, drink, and fellowship were in abundance. My dad would buy a bunch of fireworks, and the kids were allowed to pass around a lit cigar or two to light them.

There was one particular branch of the family who were greeted at these gatherings with some wariness. My Uncle Charles, his wife Shirley, and their kids would usually show up, and some kind of mayhem or disruption would almost always follow. My cousin Tommy, one of many cousins, was my own age and a regular playmate. I recall one Christmas in particular, when we were both about five or six, that when Charles and Shirley arrived, Tommy was carried into the house with his lower body—from the pelvis down—encased in a cast. He was placed on the sofa, from where he could sit and watch the fireworks outside.

Shirley explained it as a birth defect that had required surgery. That is what they told us, but I heard the women whispering in the kitchen that the boy had suffered such a brutal beating from his father that both his legs and pelvis had been broken. They also said that my cousin Eddie, another of Charles and Shirley's sons, found sticks and ashes in his stocking that morning, and later that day, one of Charles' children, Sheila, tried to set fire to the barn. She was discovered, and there was more whispering in the kitchen that the poor child was in for a savage beating when she got home.

The families regularly met at church on Sundays, after which they would visit one another for Sunday lunch on a rotating basis. My earliest memory of Sheila was encountering her in the front yard of the family's home as we drove in one time. She was probably about six years old and was standing in the yard, naked from the waist down, pissing on the ground. Ignorant of such things, I thought she was urinating out of her asshole. It seemed very strange and unnatural. Charles and Shirley had six kids: Eddie, Ronnie, Sheila, Tommy, Rhonda, and Belinda. It was around Christmas, and although it was cold, Sheila was half dressed, standing there pissing in the yard, while the others were mostly barefoot and dressed in clothes passed down from one to the other.

My uncle Charles was a slight, bespectacled man, deceptively bookish in appearance, while Shirley was a short, chain-smoking, enormously fat woman. I remember she always looked grimy, her clothes greasy and her hair lank, unwashed and loosely tied. She smelled strongly of cigarettes and body odor. Charles was a deacon in his church, so he was often better presented than she was, but he too had that pale, vitamin-deficient complexion so identifiable among white trash. It was what they used to call in the old days a "tallow" complexion, when talking about crackers, dirt-eaters, and white trash.

Their house was typical of local white trash—both then and now. As our car would round a bend along a winding dirt track and crest a rise, the first sight would be mountains of household trash out front, strewn across the earthen yard and almost extruding from the doors and windows. The house was one of those old clapboard shacks still sometimes seen along Southern roadsides, mostly derelict now, and slowly disappearing into the earth. It had no underpinning and was a typical shotgun house, where you could see straight through from the front door out the back.

Inside, as I recall, there was no heating, one naked lightbulb on the ceiling, and an atmosphere thick and pungent with the smell of piss and excrement. On a Sunday visit to one of our other aunts or uncles, we would be greeted with the smell of fried chicken and biscuits, and the warmth of a stove fire. At Charles and Shirley's place, there was never that kind of welcome—just the dank, stinking interior of a cold house, without curtains, and furnished with only a few pieces of threadbare furniture. It was a world apart.

Donald (left) stands with his coworkers Dale (center) and Jack (right) in front of a pickup truck. In his youth, Jack had operated a hidden moonshine still with a friend deep in the Lynches River Swamp of South Carolina. He often told stories of outrunning federal revenuers barefoot through the swamp—while his partner was not so fortunate, captured and sentenced to a lengthy jail term. Jack never returned to crime. After a brief stint in a cotton mill, which lasted only two weeks, he turned to steady work in construction and maintenance, remaining in that line of work until his death.

Among all my aunts and uncles, and all four of my grandparents, there was a common theme of living within the limitations of poverty while resisting a descent into the kind of conditions that Harriet Beecher Stowe wrote about in the pre–Civil War era. Charles, on the other hand, made a conscious choice to plunge straight into that life.

Charles McDowell married a woman who, even at the time, could have been regarded as a poster child of white trash, and when I knew her, she was definitely that. She was fat, crude, unkempt, uncaring, and sexually promiscuous in the careless, utilitarian way white trash women often are. They say he wanted to marry someone his parents did not approve of, and so, in rebellion, he married Shirley, and dove about as deep into white trash as it was possible to go.

Outside, meanwhile, on that particular Christmas visit, Ronnie and Eddie—both older than me—were playing with a shotgun their daddy had given them. They took turns shooting one another from a distance and then counted the welts on their backs and legs raised by the birdshot. At other times, they played on the railway line. When a train approached, they would run across a busy highway and place pennies on the rail to flatten them. One day, Tommy was hit by a car on that highway. He was thrown over the hood and into the air, landing in a heap behind. It was treated as fun, and they were back at it the next day. They did that sort of thing all the time.

Donald (right) and his brother sit with the mill's Santa Claus during the annual J.P. Stevens Industrial Mill community Christmas party. Held on a Sunday, the children came dressed in their Sunday best, reflecting both family tradition and respect for the occasion. Each child received a holiday gift bag—seen on the left—prepared according to age and gender, a gesture that brought joy to mill families during the holiday season and reinforced the sense of community within mill village life.

When she was about five or six, Belinda was also hit by a car, and killed, on Highway 49, somewhere between York and Sharon, SC, right in front of my grandparents' house. The story was sometimes told that the kids would run across the highway to reach a swimming hole on the other side. Belinda lagged a few yards behind the others and was struck, hurled up the road, and survived only a few minutes after.

While the family grieved, there were whispers that God had intervened to spare her a life of misery with her family. Maybe that was true; there were plenty of reasons to believe it might have been.

Charles, whether sincere or not, appeared content that his little girl was with Jesus. The other kids were inconsolable, especially Tommy and Sheila, who had been watching her that day. Eddie's reaction was different. His father gave him a disposable camera to record the funeral, and he did. I noticed he lingered and took many pictures of the body in the casket, and when he thought no one was looking, he touched it a few times. I always wondered about Eddie after that.

Although all the children suffered, Eddie seemed to receive particularly brutal treatment from his father. I recall one time when the septic tank backed up, and while Charles waited to see if it would clear, the family did what nature decrees out back, using a hosepipe to clean themselves. Eventually, a honey wagon was called to pump out the sewage, and since little else happened in the neighborhood, the spectacle drew a crowd. When the lid was lifted, a diabolical stench rose, and people scattered in feigned revulsion. The McDowell family became legendary in the neighborhood because of that. A baby doll belonging to Belinda was found blocking the system, and when Eddie admitted flushing it down the toilet, he was savagely beaten in full view of the gathered neighbors—the same kind of beating that likely broke Tommy's legs. Then, choking back tears, Eddie was forced to clean the shit strewn across the yard.

Violence and sexual abuse were constant themes in Charles' household. In June 1999, my mother was summoned to the Supreme Court of California to testify in support of a penalty retrial for Charles Edward McDowell Jr., who was sitting on death row for the rape and murder of Paula Rodriguez in May 1982. Charles Edward McDowell Jr., of course, was my cousin Eddie, and as the trial unfolded over several days, the full horror of what he did—and what he and his siblings had suffered at their father's hands—was exposed.

Court transcripts revealed that the defendant broke into a home in Hollywood, California, raped and murdered a housekeeper employed by the absent homeowners, and stabbed a neighbor in the neck when the man came to investigate the screams. After years off the family radar, this was the first many of us had heard of Eddie. He had already been on death row fifteen years, and his appeal sought commutation to life imprisonment.

Testimony detailed several other violent rapes, including one against a minor and another prolonged assault while an infant child was present. Sheila, Eddie's younger sister, described repeated sexual assaults by him, as did his ex-wife, whom he married in 1975 when she was fourteen. Sheila also testified that she had been abused and raped by her father over many years. The suggestion was that her brothers had also abused her. Evidence showed a hidden door built into her closet so her father could enter her room unseen. He denied intercourse but admitted masturbating and ejaculating on her.

In the hope of saving Eddie's life, family members—including my mother—testified to the horrors of his childhood. That testimony described relentless violence inflicted on Eddie and Tommy by their father, and neglect—at best—by their mother. Shirley testified that Eddie was "whipped every day" from the age of two or three. Bedwetting brought beatings and humiliation. When Ronnie wet himself, Charles pinched his penis so severely the child required surgery. When Eddie and Ronnie set their doghouse on fire, Charles stripped them naked and held them over the flames.

As the testimony continued, it became clear that Charles was not merely abusive, but monstrous. The irony was that he was a church deacon, a regular attendee, outwardly pious. Sheila testified that sexual abuse began at age three and continued until she was seventeen. And so it continued, from one lurid chapter to another, but despite it all, the sentence of death was upheld.

In January 2022, the family history darkened further. Tommy, then sixty-one, was arrested in connection with the 1986 abduction and murder of four-year-old Jessica Gutierrez in Lexington, SC. After trial, he received two life sentences. Multiple trials involving the McDowell brothers raised the spectre, not only violence and extreme abuse, but pervasive sexual exploitation.

Thomas McDowell sentenced to life in 1986 cold-case child abduction, murder of 4-year-old Lexington girl

This 2025 mugshot captures Thomas 'Tommy' McDowell, sentenced to life in prison for the 1986 cold-case abduction and murder of a 4-year-old Lexington girl—a tragic chapter finally brought to justice. Donald grew up with Tommy and his brother Eddie, who now sits on death row in California. Their story is a haunting testament to how cycles of childhood abuse and trauma, when left unaddressed, can spiral into unthinkable violence in adulthood.

SLICK LEGGING

I was standing in the most absolute
aloneness that I had ever known.
James Dickie, *Deliverance*

SOMETIME DURING HIS CHILDHOOD, Fred Pike was raped. It was a snippet of biographical detail that only came to light by accident, during a conversation on the subject of sexual misconduct in the white trash community.

"Remember that movie *Deliverance?*" He asked me. "Remember those crackers raping that fellow, what was his name, Ned Beatty, 'squeal like a pig' was the line, they say that was a dramatization, but I tell you, it weren't no such thing."

His admission, with a minimum of context, was simply that some time, when he was a child living in the Inman mill village, a relative lured him into a coal shed, and there he was gang raped by several men who were waiting. I asked him if it had happened more than once, and his reply was that he remembered only once, but probably there were more.

A lot of it, he said, was out in the open. The boys, and even the men sometimes, would visit the barn when a calf had been born and let the thing suck them like it would a cow's udder. It was a joke; it was a long-standing tradition; and although they were probably just doing what men and boys have done since the beginning of time, what was different in Fred's mind was how normal it seemed, how open it was, and how many did it. And it was not only calves but all kinds of animals, and children, of course, even one's own. That was just normal. Everyone did it.

Indeed, the greater context that Fred probably omitted from his story was how widespread the culture of violence and sexual deviancy was that Donald Williams had experienced. Years later he was surprised to learn of its commonplace nature. White trash culture has been popularized and sanitized on tv since the *Beverly Hillbillies* to *1000-Pound Sisters*; and from the *Dukes of Hazard* to *Honey-boo-boo*. And while some of the original dark traits of Ransy Sniffle might yet survive in that class, white trash culture has become mainstream and does not really exist in the same environment of introversion and extreme poverty as it once did. Perhaps a greater vigilance on the part of the police and child protection agencies has helped curb some of the more obvious excesses, along with far greater avenues of reporting, and a culture of believing victims and accusers. Either way, the abuse of one another, and one another's children, was a matter of daily routine.

There was, however, another side to the story. One of the strange anomalies of Mill Hill culture was the omnipotence of the mill bosses. The mill authorities held almost the literal power of life and death over mill communities. Since every aspect of life—from housing to education, from health to worship, and not to mention simple community—was integrated into the mill, incurring the displeasure of the mill bosses could result in the immediate and absolute removal of the means of life. There were often incidents where the mill authorities would shut the complex down to purge the ranks of their workers of anyone they found troublesome or distasteful. This would mostly be aimed at any potential industrial action, but also violence, drunkenness, or overt sexual misadventure. Most mill villages had their gangs—in Donald William's village, it was the 'Blue Buckles', and his daddy was rumored to be a member of it—and it was the job of those gangs to enforce discipline in the ranks of mill workers and their families.

The Blue Buckles, as just one example, was a gang, but not a criminal gang, perhaps more of a club or association, tasked by itself to maintain standards within the community. If, for example, a man was known to be beating his wife or children, he would be visited by a Blue Buckle member, and either warned to cease and desist, or roughed up a little bit to drive home the message. Sometimes, reports of adultery or infidelity would be heard by the local preacher, and a series of fire and brimstone services would follow, with names spoken, but more likely, a nighttime visit from the Blue Buckles. There were stories of lynchings—white on white lynchings—and others, about men caught molesting children who were tied up in barns, heaped with hay, and set on fire. It surely did happen. One time, I recall a story about the rape of a young boy by a well-known child molester who had ignored repeated warnings, and one day he was found drowned in a rain barrel with his severed penis stuffed in his mouth.

The reason that a lot of that kind of stuff happened in most of the mill communities was because the police were worthless to the community. They were corrupt and mostly indifferent to the lives and affairs within mill villages. The mills usually maintained a private security staff that was concerned solely with factory security. Typically, they were not involved in the private lives of the mill workers.

I asked Fred why so much sexual misconduct went on in those communities, and his answer was simply that folks didn't tell. They maybe reported to the Mill Hill gang, if they knew about someone outside of their family misbehaving in that way, but nothing was ever said about behavior like that going on in their own family.

"If you cause trouble." He said. "Daddy would lose his job, and we'd all be poor again. We'd go back to sharecropping, and that was nuthin' that any family wanted. If Daddy, or uncles maybe, were raping their sons and daughters, it was safer, because no one said nuthin'. A lot a folk did incest in them days. You know, in the South—they got an old saying down here—if it ain't good enough for your own family then, it ain't good enough for me."

He laughed, but it was a bitter laugh, because there was a whole lot of truth in that. You don't tell. Maybe you might have told your Mama, and even if it was someone outside the family, families would never turn each other in. The mill bosses were real sensitive to any trouble or disturbance among their workers, and any hint of misbehavior or trouble in the community and jobs were lost and folk were cast out of their homes and communities as an example to the others. Nobody reported sex crimes within a family, because not only will you have been molested, but you're now going to be hungry and homeless. These people lived day to day. Famine and hunger were always just around the corner, and that was a very real fear in those days, a very real fear.

Fred Pike's story was probably not that uncommon, and like Fred, Donald Williams suffered a similar attack at the hands of an older boy who was well known in the community for his predatory attacks against young children. Donald Williams takes up the story:

ON THE MILL HILL, SURVIVAL DEPENDED ON OBEDIENCE. The mill owners had very little tolerance for rebellion, and anyone threatening the smooth function of their operation would find themselves without a job, and that meant without a home and a community. For that reason, long before the news of any malfeasance reached the ears of a mill supervisor, the Blue Buckles handled it. Usually it was done quietly, in the shadows, with fists, clubs, and steel belt buckles. Blue Buckle justice was swift, and the loyalty of its members to the mill was unquestioned. The Blue Buckles were guardians of discipline and order, and they were tolerated by the mill bosses simply because they kept order in the ranks, which kept the machines running.

But there was another side to it. Mill Hill troublemakers and snitches did not always suffer alone. The weight of exposure and disgrace fell on an entire family, and quite often the extended family. Shame and disgrace were like a stink that permeated the community, and because the community was so tight knit, everyone knew where the smell was coming from. In an environment where order and compliance were enforced by violence, and where rumors and whispers were heard behind every door, speaking out was very often much more dangerous than just suffering in silence.

In my case, fear did not come just come from the weight of those unspoken rules, it came also from my rapist himself. His threats were unambiguous, and as a child, I believed every word he told me. He warned me he would kill me if I uttered a word, and there was no doubt in my young mind that he meant it. To illustrate his willingness to use violence, he stuffed me into a burlap sack, tied the neck, and beat me with a stick. If I cried or screamed, he warned me, he would keep beating me until I stopped, and so I did.

That's how it began, and as I reflect on it now, as an adult, I can see how he planned it. It was grooming. First the bullying, then real violence, and then rape. At the time, he was a young teenager, much older, bigger, and stronger than me, and by the time the abuse began to turn sexual, I was utterly intimidated, terrified by the sight of him, and completely under his control. That is how it goes.

Back in those days, children rarely spent their days under the supervision of parents or relatives. Things were much freer and less constrained, but also more dangerous. The mill houses were usually small, and television was limited, so kids spent a whole lot more time outside, and in and out of trouble, than they do these days. No one was ever likely to notice if a bigger boy enticed or threatened a smaller child into a shed, and no one asked at the end of the day what happened in the woods, in the churchyard, or in any one of the many hidden corners of the Mill Hill. And that is just how it happened. He took what he wanted because he knew that he could. After all, no one was watching, and because I had already figured that telling was very dangerous, no one was around to help me. The first time it happened, and the only time I will describe, was the commencement of a lifelong trauma.

First, he coaxed me into the woods behind our house, and there he told me to lie down. I was scared witless, and at the time, I had no idea what it was he wanted. Then he had me stand up, and while on my feet, he stripped me of all my clothes, using my clothes to lie on the ground as a blanket. Then had me lie down again. Then he took all his clothes off and stood above me naked. I saw his penis, with pubic hair, swollen and hard. I had seen it before because he liked to show it. He had a habit of forcing the younger boys of the neighborhood to have a pissing contest for him, to see who could piss the highest, longest, and furthest. Those contests would always end with him pulling his own penis out, making us all look at it, and then peeing on one of us.

This time, though, it was different. He did not pee on me, as I expected, but began instead to fondle himself. Then, after doing that for a while, he bent down on his knees in front of me, and pulling my legs together, he spit between them, just below my scrotum, and then slipped his penis between my legs.

They call that 'slick-legging' in the South, a term that originated in prisons. All the while, he was kissing me on my neck and cheek, although not on my lips, since he probably figured that kissing me on the mouth would make him gay, and no one in those days would admit to being gay. He kept on going, and all I can recall thinking was how much I hated it, and how heavy he was, and how hot his breath was, and how he grunted. It was terrifying and sickening. Eventually, he climaxed between my legs and on my naked torso. Afterwards, he recovered and made me play with his cum with my finger.

I have no idea how many times this happened, but it happened often. His threats to kill me and the jeopardy that I felt were real and terrifying. In time, the rapes became more experimental, and he would try stuff like putting his penis in my mouth, but I resisted, and he did not persist. I discovered before long that I was not the only one, and if luck is an applicable word, it is lucky that he did not take matters as far with me as he did with another boy. He made me watch, though, as he anally raped that boy. He made that poor kid get on his hands and knees, and he stuck his whole penis up his anus. The kid was crying and screaming, which seemed to make that rapist just go harder.

So, how did that end? My family moved on, my rapist graduated to courting women, and I passed through school, college, and a professional life. I progressed through academia, which was a rarity where I come from. He remained in the community, and I ran into him from time to time, and I still do. He is now elderly, a grandfather, and great-grandfather, a church official, and a stalwart of the community. When we meet, he will hug me, gush effusively, and tell me he loves me. Part of that, I am sure, is the knowledge that I can destroy his life with a single accusation, and that is the power that I hold over him. I have no doubt that many other young boys suffered similar abuse at his hands, and the fact that he escaped any consequence and went on to feign the respectability of a community member and esteemed churchman is really just testimony to how things were in those days.

In gathering oral testimony for this segment, I interviewed an elderly woman within my extended family group who was quite candid in what she told me. She said it went on in the family because the family kept their mouths shut, and either dealt with it or did not deal with it. Outside of the family, it was risky, but within the family, it was possible to keep such things secret, even though, often, it was an open secret. Sometimes, in church, if word got out about something going on, the pastor might preach a sermon about the evils of rape and incest, and some folks would fidget in their pews, and maybe go home and pray, and keep off their sisters for a while, but mainly it was just a way to keep it all quiet. A lot of those folks went to church, and a lot of those preachers were doing just the same thing.

She told me that all her brothers and sisters were regularly raped, mostly by uncles, but also by one brother in particular who would then go on to freely rape and molest his own sons and daughters. My own cousin Eddie, my uncle Charles` eldest son, was repeatedly raped by his father, and his relatives on his mother`s side. I remember that those guys were like the cast of *Deliverance*. Charles was born into the mill culture, like all the rest, but he married into white trash, real white trash, and he jumped into that world with both feet. Some of his mother's brothers picked on Eddie in particular, and I recall it being said that one would hold the poor kid down while the others anally raped him. They did not seem to make any effort to hide it, and it went on until Eddie eventually ran away from home.

I discovered years later, when I was teaching, that one of those men was also raping his own daughter. She was a student of mine at the time, and her story was yet another of a young girl molested by her father, falling pregnant by him, and then giving birth to a little girl who also fell victim to her father, who was also her grandfather. Such things were not that uncommon. These men were all classic white trash.

People have asked me how men like my rapist, Eddie`s rapists, Uncle Charles, and all of those like him, learned that type of behavior. It is a strange thing that York, SC, which is where most of the family resided, was a well-known center of homosexual activity. Part of the reason for this was the fact that it was the winter headquarters of the Wallace Brothers Circus, later Barnett`s (a famous landmark in the city is the burial site of an elephant), and I guess with the long winter sojourn of a lot of circus and funfair folk, local boys, with such predilections, could find partners and teachers. That`s what they say, anyway, although that kind of behavior was so widespread the circus folk could not take all the blame.

There was also a pretty famous whorehouse on the edge of the city limit in York, SC, known as Miss Hattie`s, and maybe there was more than one, but either way, that was the university of sex back in those days. I recall a kid at school who talked for months about saving his money and losing his virginity at Hattie`s. When the day came, and he had enough money, he went by, paid his money and told the madame what he wanted. She directed him upstairs to a room, and told him to knock, and his girl would be there. He went upstairs and knocked and the woman who opened the door was his mother.

Fred Pike told the story of once visiting the burlesque with Dennis Pike, Jason Pike's father: "We played hooky together, going down New Prospect to shoot basketball. We go down one Monday every month, go down to a burlesque show. In those days, it was kinda like a bikini, ain`t like now where you got gashes all over the place. We`d go down to the burlesque show, and I looked down four rows and there was my damn daddy down there, `ol bald head. He walked up the aisle and we made eye contact. He went to his grave and never mentioned that to me, and I never mentioned it to him neither."

A famous story related to Hattie`s establishment comes from Donald's brother when he was a young man in the 1970s. He was working for York Concrete, and they had done some work for Hattie, and they sent him to collect some money. At the time, the business was fronted by a legitimate truck stop, and he walked in and was met by a short, thickset, heavy-breasted woman standing behind the food counter cooking on a griddle. He introduced himself, and she said, "Son, have a seat, I`m Hattie."

He was talking to the infamous Hattie, and he said, "I`m here to collect this money."

She said, "Well, wait just a minute."

When that minute passed, she placed a plate of breakfast in front of him, and he said, "Ma`am, I didn`t order any breakfast!"

"I don`t care," she replied, "I`m a`cookin` fer yer, now jus` go ahead and eat."

In the process, she hauled out her breasts and laid them down on the table, and said – "Whad`ya think of these great big titties?"

I guess he said they were fine, and she told him then, after he`d finished up his breakfast, to go upstairs and one of those girls over there that was playing pool would come up and take care of him for free – "Since y`all did this work for me."

He looked over, and there were three girls playing pool at a table, and one of them was a girl he went to school with. I don`t know whether he did or didn`t, but he swears he didn`t, but hell, who knows?

A Problem of Degeneracy

Karl Marx, The Communist Manifesto

THE EIGHTEENTH AND NINETEENTH CENTURIES IN THE UNITED STATES, like everywhere else in the western world, was an era of rapid political, scientific, artistic and technological advance. It marked the commencement of the Age of Enlightenment;

the American and French revolutions; the Haitian Revolution; the rise of secularism and democracy; the abolition of slavery in the British Empire and the vaulting advances made by the Industrial Revolution. In 1776, *The Wealth of Nations* was published; 1848, the *Communist Manifesto*; *Das Kapital* two decades later, and in between, Charles Darwin`s *Origin of the Species*. The established world order, in place since the fall of the Roman Empire, was suddenly confronted by a revolutionary storm of new concepts and ideas.

Among those new ideas and disciplines were the twin sciences of sociology and anthropology, which completely altered how society viewed itself. Alongside the great moral dilemma posed to the new republic by that `peculiar institution`, lay another inescapable blight on the cultural landscape of the South: white poverty.

Yes, indeed. By the outbreak of the Civil War, and even more so at its conclusion, the population of those known variously as lubbers, crackers, sandhillers and dirt-eaters, exploded to such an extent that their presence could no longer reasonably be ignored. Most of those whites living in extreme poverty in the South were derived from ancestors who had either tried to escape the serfdom of a feudal system of land ownership only to find themselves as bonded labor in the new ways of doing things. This hang over plantation system of slavery disguised in the legitimacy of industry managed captive labor on an industrial scale to the great estates of the South. This had the immediate effect of more deeply impoverishing landless whites. As Harriet Beecher-Stowe remarked, why hire a white carpenter if you already own a black one, and why hire white labor when black labor was free? Obviously, this is a simplistic view of it, but it was a principle that nonetheless deeply impacted that class of landless whites trying to survive in a labor market dominated by slavery.

Two young boys stand proudly on a weathered wooden porch, clad in humble attire, evoking the simplicity of rural life in a bygone era. The boy on the left may have suffered from a hookworm infestation, a condition that likely stunted his growth.

Then there was that age-old, philosophical issue that also influenced the condition of poor whites in that era, and that was the binary issue of race. The general worldview at the time was that the European, Anglo-Saxon race stood at the pinnacle of race hierarchy in the world, and the negro languished at the bottom. That made it a whole lot easier to enslave an entire race if its status in life was defined by slavery. Just as an example, the North African term used to describe black, sub-Saharan Africans was, and still is in many places, *Abid*, which means slave, suggesting that black Africans belonged in that condition, and were defined by it. Whites, whose social condition was manifestly lower than blacks in the Southern states, could only claim superiority by eschewing the manual labor that blacks undertook as slaves, and so wage labor became a dirty word among them. Many preferred to live a feral, nomadic existence as virtual hunter-gatherers than to be seen to labor alongside an inferior class of people. That was all they had to separate themselves from those whose black skin, scarred backs, and calloused hands identified them as inferior. Thus, no matter how degraded and impoverished those dirt-eaters were, they were not black, and so they at least belonged to the superior race.

As those emerging sociologists and anthropologists began to look more closely at the lubbers and sandhillers of the Carolinas, they were forced to acknowledge that this ever-growing subculture of white people was, in practical terms, inferior to the black man, and that was not an easy idea to digest. Indeed, it implied a very contradictory, epoch-changing state of affairs.

If a white skin suggested purity and godliness, as many would swear that it did, since it was only the black man`s absence of soul that justified his enslavement, then poor white trash implied an ungodly, desacralized state of corrupted whiteness. During the eighteenth and early nineteenth centuries, and even earlier still, the lubbers and their kin had simply been an object of ridicule, satire, and lip-curling social commentary. However, as the great race issue was settled in the crucible of civil war, and the black man was released into the world as an equal, the question of that lingering culture of white degradation came much more to the fore. A culture of contempt had leaned toward becoming one of intellectual curiosity and concern.

Also, in the late nineteenth and early twentieth centuries, there emerged the concept of eugenics, riding somewhat on the coattails of the publication of Darwin`s *Origin of the Species*.[6] It thereafter became difficult to escape the reality that fair-skinned people of Anglo-Saxon origin were not automatically superior, but in many cases, certainly in

---

[6] It was Darwin's younger half-cousin Francis Galton who founded the science of eugenics and not Darwin himself, which is a point worth noting.

the southern states, noticeably inferior to blacks and native Americans, and that was not a comfortable idea.

Although there were competing arguments put forward around the pros and cons of slavery, generally, it was agreed by all sides that the problem was not the influence of slavery on white culture, but simply *tainted blood*. The same tainted blood that had encouraged the original expatriation of these waste people to America. The blood of some whites was tainted, and this being the case, no quantum shifts in the social order, like the abolition of slavery, were ever likely to make the slightest difference. In fact, releasing a generation of skilled blacks into the wage laboring class simply disadvantaged whites even further. The answer, many believed, lay in a more direct and aggressive approach. Where once it was a term confined to vernacular use among blacks, 'poor white trash' now entered the established national dictionary, creating a real conundrum for the superior classes.

This was an interesting pivot in history. While I am no scholar of history, even I can see that it marked a turning point in the general attitude of the white nation toward its feeble-minded and morally degenerate brethren.

The ideological objective of eugenics was the improvement of the genetic quality of the human population by promoting the reproduction of people with desirable traits, or positive eugenics, and intervening to limit or prevent the reproduction of those considered to have undesirable traits, or negative eugenics. Eugenicists held the view that traits such as intelligence, criminality, and mental illness were inherited, and they sought to use selective breeding to build an ideal society.

As I was digging into the back story of the eugenics movement, I stumbled on a compendium of studies undertaken about the turn of the twentieth century. These studies sought collectively to reinforce some of the dogma used to justify things like forced sterilization and marriage laws. Reading through some of the case studies, I was struck by how familiar many of the themes sounded, reflecting on people, and families, not least my own, that I knew, and that displayed a lot of these essential characteristics.

The first of these studies, conducted by Richard L. Dugdale in the 1870s, involved a family known as the Jukes, which purported to show that the descendants of this family were genetically predisposed to crime, poverty, and social deviance.

While inspecting prisons in New York, Richard Dugdale noticed that a good number of the prisoners seemed to be related, tracing their ancestry back to a man known as Max, an apparent Dutch immigrant born around 1720. Max was a criminal who arrived in the American colonies just a few steps ahead of the Dutch law. Dugdale's study concluded that, among 1,200 descendants of Max, a significant proportion had also been criminals, paupers, prostitutes, imbeciles, or anyone else dependent on public welfare. He advanced the argument that the family's many social problems resulted from hereditary factors, combined with poor environmental conditions. The purpose of this study was initially to highlight the need for social reform and better environmental conditions to prevent crime and poverty, but the work was later co-opted by eugenicists who saw it as proof that undesirable traits were primarily inherited.

Before we get into how the eugenics movement impacted the white trash phenomenon, it would probably be enlightening to extract a few passages from Dugdale's study of the Jukes, and a few others included in the collection. These were all, in one way or another, used to bolster the conclusions and work of the eugenics movement.

The pseudo-scientific nature of the Jukes study is evident from the onset, but what is interesting is how some snippets of description give color to a class of people much more prevalent in those days than these. Let me give you an example:

The impudicity of `the Juke` women is twenty-nine times greater than the average of women, and, as a result, one fourth of the children are illegitimate, not few of them being born during the imprisonment of the husband.

This conforms very well to what has been said of my own family, and it is a common enough observation. Donald Williams remarked that there seemed to be a fire in the pants of all the women of his family, and there certainly was a lot of heat in the pants of the women of my own. Syphilis is something that is widely discussed and observed in all the various studies. It seems that a lot of the general stupor and idleness that characterized the white trash of that era can justifiably be attributed to the effects of this disease, and no doubt, many others. Prostitution was a common occupation among women, and several examples are cited of the daughters of a family running brothels in their own homes—those homes being the usual hovels that are so variously described. Seventy-nine percent of those Jukes studied, male and female, young and old, displayed symptoms of syphilis.

> *The eldest daughter of Hans is weak-minded and blind, married to a man who is also weak-minded and blind, and she transmits, in the form of premature death, to six out of her eight children, the syphilis she has inherited in the form of imbecility and blindness; the vitality of her two surviving daughters being impaired.*

Incidentally, Hans was a veteran of the War of 1812 and spent most of his life either in the poor house or in prison. Following his family line, Dugdale makes this observation:

> *With licentiousness hereditary and wasting the energies, with such a disease entailed and slowly consuming the life, it is not too much to say that the slothful habits are due to an under-vitalized condition, which is only deferred death; while at other points disease smites with a stronger hand, and makes a fool or makes an infant corpse, leaving the surviving progeny weak and crippled, capable only of bringing forth a posterity of dependents to recruit the procession of woe on its way to extinction.*

The complete study of the Jukes followed in a similar vein. It painted a morbid picture of moral depletion, disease, physical frailty, and mental weakness, passed from one generation to the other, which tended to confirm Dugdale's hypothesis that such traits and frailties were hereditary. Feeble-mindedness was a common theme, as was consanguinity and incest. I will not bore the reader with any more repetitions of the same story, other than to note that such poverty and social decay must have been so widespread at that time that it demanded some coordinated societal response. That social response, at least in part, was the emergence of the eugenics movement, which identified the problem as one of degeneracy, and sought ways to deal with it. There was a sense that people thus described should be limited in their ability to vote—since a white trash vote went to whoever was supplying the liquor—go to school, or in any way participate in the normal functions of civil society. We need not get too caught up in the history of social Darwinism and how the theory of natural selection influenced eugenics, other than to observe that human characteristics, especially intelligence and moral character were regarded as biologically transmissible and inheritable.[7] In 1910, Eugenics research was formalized under the umbrella of the Eugenics Research Office, funded in part by the Carnegie Foundation, and Aunt Jo-lyn Harriman, the wife of the famous railroad magnate Edward Harriman. A center for the study of human evolution was established in Cold Spring Harbor, Long Island, which soon became the epicenter of eugenics research in the United States.

Much of the focus of this research was racial, contemplating the seemingly unequal endowments of various races. This was intended, probably, to underpin a sense that black citizens of the United States occupied some inferior status on the ladder of human capability and ought to be treated as such and so be assigned a lesser status. The issue of white trash was more confusing because obviously the *white* part of

---

[7] Wray, Matt. *Not Quite White: White Trash and the Boundaries of Whiteness* (p. 69). Duke University Press.

the white trash label should have implied some identifiable superiority, but it did not. In most cases it was obvious to anyone that the broad sweep of white trash could be judged at first glance to be mostly inferior in lifestyle and achievements to blacks. Strategies to bleach out this stain took on various forms, including placing restrictions on incoming immigration, mandating the institutionalization of, and legalizing the involuntary sterilization of the biologically unfit, all with the unspoken objective of creating a superior race, and then protecting it.

As the superior class thought about this problem, scratching their heads for solutions, they faced two significant concerns. First was the cost of dealing with the problem through charity and social welfare, and the second was the cost in terms of public health in the unregulated reproduction of this undesirable class. It was believed that, if left unchecked, this class would endlessly replicate its diseased genetic material and spread its vice and immorality throughout the community and the nation. A far better, if somewhat controversial solution, was involuntary sterilization.

The eugenics movement was steeped in a little bit of science, and a whole lot of pseudo-science. The movement was international, and as we all know, it peaked in infamy during the 1930s in Germany.

Yes indeed. Although the eugenics movement was never quite as widespread and militant in the United States as it was in Germany, it did emerge during an era of mass migration, with people of different origins and complexions flooding into the country from all over the world. And while a whole lot of anxiety was generated over the purity of the Anglo-Saxon race in the United States, it was the enemy within that caused the most hand-wringing and pearl-clutching among the white social elites and intelligentsia. That enemy was the white trash— the idiots, morons, and high-grade defectives—known collectively as the feeble-minded, who threatened by their mere presence to degrade the genetic integrity of the mass of working whites.

NAVY DEPARTMENT
Commission on Training Camp Activities. Social Hygiene Division

Venereal Diseases

Gonorrhea
(Clap, dose, chordee, stricture.)

A germ disease that causes:

Chronic ill health

Many childless marriages

Serious operations on vital organs of women

Diseases of joints, bladder and generative organs

Much blindness among babies

Syphilis
(Pox, syph, old case, etc.)

A blood disease that causes:

Insanity

Paresis or softening of brain

Locomotor ataxia

Paralysis in early life

Imbecile and crippled children

Diseases of heart, blood vessels, etc.

BOTH these diseases can be cured, but they are often not cured, even after all signs disappear under treatment—a real cure is a matter of months and sometimes years. Practically all prostitutes have one or both.

Chancroid—[soft chancre, haircut, burn, etc]. A germ disease that causes large sores on the sex organs. The most frequent cause of buboes [*blue balls.*] Dangerous because syphilis often masquerades as chancroid.

HOW TO PREVENT THEM
① Keep away from prostitutes and all "easy women"—almost all are diseased.
② Control your sex impulses—you don't need sexual intercourse to be healthy.

BEWARE OF ADVERTISING DOCTORS

If you *have* or ever have had Gonorrhea or Syphilis

Do this: Go immediately to your medical officer. Get a thorough examination. Find out what is the matter with you. Then determine to be cured, even if it takes years to do it.

Don't Go to doctors who advertise (specialists in men's diseases, nervous debility, etc.) All that these quacks want is your money. Don't try to treat yourself with patent medicines.

YOUR MEDICAL OFFICER
will be glad to give you friendly advice about the true facts of sex and the venereal diseases

Issued by the Navy Department's Commission on Training Camp Activities, Social Hygiene Division, this poster warned sailors about the dangers of gonorrhea, syphilis, and chancroid during World War I. It outlined the severe health consequences of untreated infections, from blindness and sterility to paralysis and mental illness. The notice emphasized prevention, urging men to avoid prostitutes, control sexual impulses, and seek immediate medical treatment if exposed. It also cautioned against fraudulent "advertising doctors" who profited from unproven cures. Such posters were part of a larger federal campaign to protect military readiness by reducing sexually transmitted diseases among servicemen—a leading cause of lost manpower during the war.

A Problem of Degeneracy

In 1927, the United States Supreme Court ruled in a majority opinion that a state statute authorizing compulsory sterilization of the unfit, including the intellectually disabled, 'for the protection and health of the state, was not in violation of the Due Process clause of the Fourteenth Amendment. Variations of the statute were drafted in different states, and I was surprised to discover that, as late as 1981, legislation was passed authorizing the involuntary sterilization of an idiot if it was in his or her best interest.

All this, however, is just is the long way to getting round to saying that, when the establishment began to take stock of rural poverty, and started to appreciate its scope, and its cause and effect, the great and the good among them concluded that digging up the roots would make more sense than hacking at the branches. General guidelines were put in place, and a program was launched. It was slow to start, but it gathered momentum quickly. Standard systems were developed to identify those troublesome morons, idiots and the feeble-minded, and by following the branches of the family tree, the entire problem could relatively easily be nipped in the bud.

If Darwin's theory of natural selection was true, then evolution would inevitably, one day, arrive at perfection. The eugenics movement comprised many who believed in Darwin's theory with almost religious fervor, and their objective in deciding who could reproduce and who could not was no different from any cattle breeder's—to produce an immaculate society of uniformly perfect specimens. Although statistics vary, the accepted total of people involuntarily sterilized in the United States stands at 70,000. I do not believe that this total cut too deeply into the populations of white trash in the South, but it certainly showed that society was looking at the problem in a different way.

THE GERM OF LAZINESS

IN 1877, THE SAME YEAR THAT RICHARD DUGDALE published his groundbreaking study of the Juke family, Italian scientists established a principal for diagnosing hookworm infestation, which set in motion a completely different approach to dealing with the crisis of those 'low-life, uneducated poor'.

Some of the pseudo-scientific terms used at the time to describe those 'low-life, uneducated poor', otherwise known as the feeble-minded, would boggle the mind today. Among them were: *idiot, low-grade imbecile, medium-grade imbecile, high-grade imbecile* and *moron*, the latter capable of some work requiring reason and the former able to manage only limited functions of self-preservation. The key point, however, is that the feebleminded were seen as not only lacking basic intelligence, but also moral capacity. Therefore, the decision to interfere with their ability to reproduce was seen as a rampart against any potential for the disease of their existence to spread. As a policy, though, forced sterilization was always likely to have a limited effect, and although laws were passed in most states through the 1930s legalizing its practice, it was always to be regarded by the enlightened with a little bit of moral discomfort. How it impacted the actual numbers of white trash is hard to say, although it certainly did put an effective stop to a lot of breeding.

Parallel to the eugenics movement ran a much more practical and enlightened policy, an early campaign in public health, that targeted the hookworm. In 1908, President Theodore Roosevelt appointed a commission to study the conditions of rural life in America. This commission was part of a wider program known as the *Country Life Movement*, which was broadly mandated to try and improve the conditions of rural life, mainly across the impoverished southern reaches of the country.

This patent medicine ad promoted "Mother Swan's Worm Syrup" as a remedy for childhood ailments such as feverishness, restlessness, constipation, and especially intestinal worms. Marketed as "perfectly harmless" and "the most effective worm destroyer extant," the syrup promised safety, sweetness, and gentle cathartic effects. Products like this were widely sold in the United States before modern regulations, reflecting both the prevalence of parasitic infections—such as hookworm—and the popularity of over-the-counter "cures" prior to the establishment of the Pure Food and Drug Act of 1906.

As the story goes, three members of the commission were seated in the smoking compartment of a train travelling through the South, reflecting on what they referred to as 'this land of forgotten men and women'. The three were Henry Wallace, future vice-President under Franklin D Roosevelt, and a man dedicated to the relief of rural poverty; Walter Page, journalist and social reformer, and Dr. Charles Wardell Stiles, an eminent parasitologist.

When Wallace saw his first specimen of a Carolina sandhiller, a modern Ransy Sniffle, leaning against the stationhouse wall of a small railroad town, he was astonished.

"What is *that*?" He asked.

"That." Walter Page replied. " Is a so called 'poor white'."

"That man is a dirteater." Added Stiles. "His condition is due to hookworm infection; he can be cured at a cost of about fifty cents for drugs, and in a few weeks time, he can be turned into a useful man."[8]

The hookworm, Stiles went on to explain, was, and still is, a parasite picked up in larval form mostly by children who spent their days barefoot. It quickly bores through the skin, in the soft areas between the toes, eventually moving into the bloodstream eventually arriving at the lungs. From there, it is coughed up, and then swallowed, swiftly colonizing the stomach and the small intestine. Once there, it attaches to the intestinal membrane, feeding off the host's blood, and reproducing at an astronomical rate. The eggs are passed out along with the hosts feces, where they hatch and infect the surrounding soil, waiting for a passing, barefoot human.

At that time, as many as two million Southerners were thought to be infected, most of them poor whites. The main symptom of severe infection was acute anemia and a subsequent susceptibility to other conditions, like tuberculosis or pneumonia. More practically, it led to lethargy, weakness, brain fog, and the consequent idleness of folk too debilitated to rise to much.

To Stiles' two companions, this was a world-altering revelation. If the disease of laziness so rampant in the South could be cured by fifty cents' worth of drugs, would that price not be more than justified by the explosion of productivity likely when two-thirds of the working population could be cured of their apparent idleness?

Soon afterward, Walter Page arranged for Dr. Stiles to present this opinion to the director of philanthropies in the offices of John D Rockefeller, and within a few months, the *Rockefeller Sanitary*

---

[8] Facing South, *The Great Hookworm Crusade*, Allen Tullos, 1976.

Commission for the Eradication of Hookworm Disease was formed, with one million dollars of Rockefeller money pledged for five years` work.[9]

IMPORTANT!
HOOKWORM DISEASE
TREATED FREE

Durham County Commissioners, co-operating with the State Board of Health, will conduct temporary Dispensaries for the examination and treatment of Hookworm disease. These Dispensaries will be free to all from 9:30 A. M. to 3:30 P. M. at the following places:

Bahama, Tuesdays, November 18, 25; December 2, 9, 16, 23.
Massys' Chapel, Wednesdays, November 19, 26; December 3, 10, 17, 24.
East Durham, Thursdays, November 20; December 4, 11, 18.
West Durham, Fridays, November 21, 28; December 5, 12, 19, 26.
Durham, Saturdays, November 22, 29; December 6, 13, 20, 27.

Dr. H. L. SLOAN, of the State Board of Health, and District Director for Hookworm Disease, will be in charge of these Dispensaries, assisted by Mr. W. S. Tuttle, Microscopist. Lectures on Hookworm Disease and Sanitation will be delivered daily. You can see at the Dispensary all kinds of worms and pictures of people before and after treatment.

This public health poster announces the establishment of free dispensaries for the treatment of hookworm disease, sponsored by the Durham County Commissioners in cooperation with the North Carolina State Board of Health. The clinics were scheduled at churches and community centers across the county, offering examinations and remedies between November and December. Under the direction of Dr. H. L. Sloan, State Director for Hookworm Disease, the campaign also featured lectures on prevention and sanitation, as well as before-and-after images of patients. This notice reflects the widespread effort of the Rockefeller Sanitary Commission (1909–1914) and local health authorities to combat hookworm in the South, aiming to improve both public health and economic productivity.

AS I WAS READING THROUGH CHARLES STILES` memoirs and clinical notes, I was struck by the fact that here is an all-American

---

[9] Charles W. Stiles, *Early History, in Part Esoteric, of the Hookworm (Uncinariasis) Campaign in Our Southern United States,* The Journal of Parasitology, XXV (August, 1939), p. 300. Aunt Jo-lyn Boccaccio, "Ground Itch and Dew Poison: The Rockefeller Sanitary Commission 1909-1914," Journal of the History of Medicine and Allied Sciences, XXVII (January, 1972), p. 81.

hero who labored in anonymity, and never won, or even sought, the recognition that he deserved for such a huge contribution to American health and productivity.

Stiles spent his early adulthood as a medical missionary serving the New York Methodist Church, studying medical zoology at various European universities. He thus made the acquaintance of Ancylostoma *duodenale, or* the Old-World hookworm, known to be the cause of severe anemia among bricklayers, tunnel workers and miners. By correlating both climate and soil conditions, he figured that the same parasite was probably at the root of many of the same symptoms suffered by the rural poor of the American South.

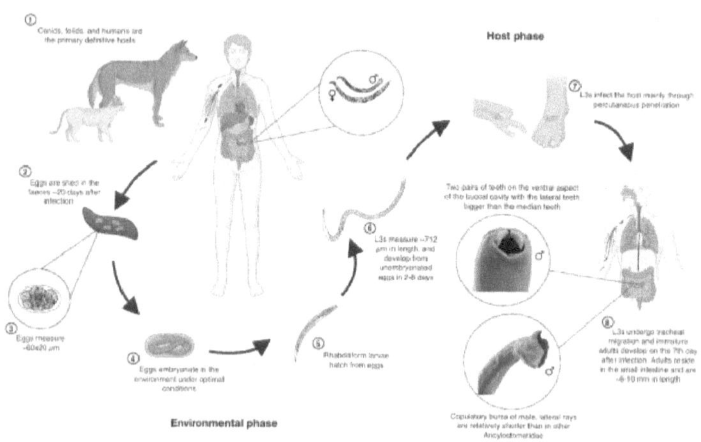

In the early 20th century, hookworm infestation plagued much of the American South, particularly in poor rural areas with warm, moist climates and inadequate sanitation. Spread through bare feet and contaminated soil, hookworms caused widespread anemia, fatigue, and developmental delays, especially among children. These effects severely hindered school attendance, work productivity, and overall health—earning the South the grim nickname 'The Germ-Ridden Region.' It wasn't until public health campaigns in the 1910s, led by organizations like the Rockefeller Sanitary Commission, that mass deworming treatments, improved sanitation, and public education efforts began breaking the cycle. Understanding the parasite's lifecycle, as illustrated here, was key to changing behaviors and lifting entire communities out of a cycle of illness and poverty.

Back home in the United States, his initial investigations failed to yield much, mainly because of the resistance he encountered from crackers and sandhillers who were deeply suspicious of a Yankee doctor looking to collect samples of their feces. What could this mean, many a superstitious sandhiller asked themselves? No good ever came of a Yankee doctor.

Stiles was able, however, to obtain a few samples from Texas and Puerto Rico, and from those he discovered an entirely new species of hookworm that he named *Necator americanus*, or the 'American murderer'. A few years later, the same species was discovered among African natives, which seemed like pretty clear evidence that the parasite had been introduced to the Americas through the slave trade.

In recent years, there have been disputes about this origin theory, but either way, Stiles was probably the first to notice, once he had discovered them, that the symptoms of hookworm infestation were widespread, and almost universal among that despised class of poor whites. It was at the root of that distinctive pallor, those jaundiced eyes, but most importantly, that complete disinterest in labor that so characterized the life and times of a cracker.

Another detail that Stiles was aware of, thanks to his European experience, was the fact that hookworm infestation and the condition known as *pica*, were very closely allied. For the sake of those who do not know what pica is, it is the underlying condition related to dirt eating, and everyone knows that dirt-eaters have epitomized white trash since the earliest recognition of their existence.

Pica is described as the craving or consumption of objects that are not normally intended to be consumed. Throughout his life, my daddy was known to eat pencils, to the extent that, when he retired, his colleagues presented him with a plaque decorated with a bunch of chewed-up pencils, since that was his most conspicuous habit. Fred Pike theorized that the habit was prompted by malnutrition and hunger as a child, and that is probably true, because he was known to eat tree bark and resin, and probably he ate dirt too. The cause and effect of pica are still being debated, and although the dirt-eating habit of Southern white trash still has folk scratching their heads, the assumption has tended to be that mineral deficiencies lie at the root of it. Hookworm causes chronic anemia, and there has long been the supposition that red clays are preferred because of their iron content. White, kaolin-type soils are another favorite because, as a binding agent, they apparently help draw poisons out of the body. Either way, hookworm infestation and dirt-eating were so closely allied that Stiles could be fairly certain that in regions where dirt-eating was common, hookworm infestation was likely to be just as common.

In the past, the condition of poor Southern whites was attributed to bad breeding and inferior stock, disrupting the treasured notion of white superiority. It would probably have come as a relief to many to learn that it was not racial inferiority, but just a disease imported inadvertently by African slaves.

One of the problems with hookworm infestation was, and is, that it lacks dramatic symptoms, like malaria or yellow fever. Instead, it manifests just a slow and insidious creep of mental and physical malaise, as well as an enhanced susceptibility to other diseases, like tuberculosis and pneumonia.

According to the Rockefeller Foundation Annual Report of 1915: *This disease is never spectacular, like yellow fever or plague or pernicious malaria. It is the greater menace because it works subtly…hookworm disease, working so insidiously as frequently to escape the attention even of its victims, tends to weaken the [human] race by sapping its vitality.*

It was difficult, then, to get anyone to take Styles seriously. This, however, changed quite spectacularly one evening in December 1902, when Charles Stiles, who was a plain-speaking character, delivered an address to a convention of physicians and sanitarians in Washington DC. His position at the time was described as *Chief of the Division of Zoology of the United States Public Health Service.*

Generally, the response to his appeal was tepid, and with his monotonous delivery and generally uninteresting character, he failed to excite much interest from his audience. There was, however, a young journalist in the audience who as the story goes, listened to the symptoms of hookworm infection, or *uncinariasis*, and wondered if it might explain his own listlessness and frequent narcolepsy. He left the auditorium, went back home, and there sat down to compose a piece for the New York *Sun*.

The article appeared the next morning under the banner headline *Germ of Laziness Found: Disease of the Crackers and Some Nations Identified*. According to the *Sun*, Stiles declared that the presence of hookworm in the South had caused: *The pitiable condition of the poor whites. Its presence in succeeding generations had resulted in their inferior physical development and mental powers and is the cause of the proverbial laziness of the 'cracker'.*

The article triggered an explosion of satire and humor, prompting facetious articles and a torrent of cartoons. It also, however, served to thrust the issue to the forefront of public consciousness. As a preventive medicine officer in the US Army, I found this story very interesting, particularly the fact that it began a virtual revolution in public medicine, emphasizing prevention as the most effective cure. It also explained a lot of Southern history, and it might even have been at the root of the weakened physicality of Confederate troops during the Civil War. Committed Rebels scoffed at that idea, pointing out that it usually took five Yankees to bring down a single Rebel, which is probably not true at all. One particular piece of press doggerel was published in the British journal *Truth*:

> *I for long had believed that, concerning my case,*
> *There existed much popular haziness;*
> *I for years felt it was grossly unfair*
> *To regard as my failing my laziness;*
> *Now, the truth has come out, thanks to good Doctor Stiles,*
> *And 'tis proved how unjust a strong bias is,*
> *For I, if you please, for my idleness scorned,*
> *Have been suffering from uncinariasis!*

The country south of the Mason-Dixon line was always notoriously unhealthy. In the days before public health, it was malaria country, and if the sandy soils of the Carolina coastal plain were ideal for nurturing the hookworm larvae, the enervating climate was certainly ideally suited for the advance of any tropical disease. From the earliest days of the southern colonies, sickness was a fact of life, and high infant mortality rates and lower life expectancy were all just realities of Southern life.

The humor that was generated by the *Germ of Laziness* article, despite bringing the issue to the forefront of public consciousness, made it difficult for many to really take seriously. Congress, studiously alert to pests and parasites in crops and livestock, showed no interest in funding a public health program in the South. Stiles realized he would need to court private wealth, and it was the *Commission on Country Life*, and that serendipitous encounter on a Southern train platform, that provided the link to Rockefeller money, and the rest, of course, is history.

During the first year of the work, the Rockefeller Sanitary Commission examined north of 100,000 souls in nine Southern states, finding among them 43,000 infested with hookworm. In poorer districts, the rates of infestation ran to about ninety percent, and of those, most were the few children within a family who were well enough to go to school. Everyone, children, parents, and teachers, were treated with a combination of thymol and Epsom salts—the former to cause the worms to slacken their grip on the intestinal walls of the patient and the latter to purge the intestines to flush them out.

A group of people, including children, stands proudly before a "County Dispensary for Free Treatment of Hookworm Disease" banner, reflecting early 20th-century public health efforts.

A year later, a teacher was interviewed, and her comment was: "Children who, before the treatment, were listless and dull and are now active and alert; children who would not study a year ago are not only studying now but are finding a joy in learning. They have a new outlook on life. There is a new spirit in the school. Most of the forty-five who were sick at home are now well and coming to school."[10]

It is hard to overstate how incredibly dramatic the effect of the *Great Hookworm Crusade* was. It was probably comparable to how a drop of fresh lemon juice eradicated scurvy, how quinine conquered malaria, or even the discovery of penicillin. The information campaign that ran parallel to testing and treatment helped dispel superstition and drove forward the science of public health and sanitation. Preventive techniques were introduced, like the introduction of toilets and privies, an emphasis on the wearing of shoes, and the encouragement of practices that helped limit the direct pollution of the soil by indiscriminate defecation around the homestead.

---

[10] Sullivan, Mark. *Our times : 1900-1925. III, Pre-war America*, 1971, p330

Just these dramatic results themselves helped to convince the public of the good that was being done, and very quickly, rural clinics and treatment centers moved from having to trick and coerce country dwellers to visit, to being overwhelmed. Public health and preventive medicine moved much closer to the center of medical doctrine. Almost overnight, the widespread picture of wasted, listless people and rickety, malnourished children disappeared. While eugenics and forced sterilization might have mopped up the stragglers and cleaned up the landscape, it was the hookworm crusade that removed the widespread spectacle of deep poverty in the South.

Just by way of statistics, by 1914, half a million school children and 400,000 adults had been tested, with more than 380,000 treated and cured. The public health campaign helped put a stop to fresh infestation, and with a population now conscious of the cause and effect, treatment was usually promptly sought if symptoms were identified. Thanks to medical examinations given to men joining the military, and to the many thousands of returning WW1 soldiers huge numbers of cases were discovered. These were all promptly treated, bringing the total of successful treatments up to about seven million by the end of the 1920s.

This cartoon depicts philanthropist John D. Rockefeller confronting the "Hookworm" with his immense wealth. Rockefeller, holding a brush labeled "John D.," prepares to scrub out the parasite as money labeled "One Million Dollars" pours into the fight. The image references Rockefeller's $1 million donation that launched the Rockefeller Sanitary Commission (1909– 1914), a major public health campaign to eradicate hookworm across the American South. Borne's cartoon underscores both the scale of the problem and the unprecedented private investment directed toward improving Southern health and productivity.

The Roaring Twenties were generally an era of growth and prosperity in the United States. The South had begun to regain its economic foothold along with the rest of the country as a rising tide floats all ships. The image of dire poverty in the South was becoming considered a fringe condition. On October 29, 1929 this tide of prosperity reversed and the image of deep poverty in America became universal reality.

BLOODY THURSDAY

NO ONE QUITE KNEW WHO MY GRANDADDY WAS, but in and out of my daddy's life drifted old Hamp Pike. Dad had a faded group picture that showed Hamp in the company of a handful of rusticated looking men, standing alongside an old downtown building somewhere, maybe a bar. It looked a like a desert setting, so maybe it was taken someplace in Arizona, or Nevada, or maybe even Texas. While the others were dressed in denim dungarees, Hamp was wearing a well-tailored jacket, an open neck shirt and a pair of flowing slacks. On his head, shading his eyes, was a fedora hat, and his hands were casually thrust into his pockets. It looked like the picture had been taken sometime in the 1950s. Hamp was a tall, rangy-looking man, somewhat like Ralph, relaxed in posture, and with a friendly, engaging smile.

Whenever my dad had a yarn to spin that required a grasshopper-and-ant moral, he would revive the character of Hamp Pike, telling stories of his shiftless ambulation through the South during the Depression Era. Hamp was an example of how a rolling stone gathered no moss, and how, in contrast, my daddy's own history of diligent toil and careful career management projected him to a place of security and comfort. The Ant and the Grasshopper, of course, were characters in one of Aesop's Fables. It told the story of the Grasshopper, who frolicked, danced, and sang all summer, while the ant worked diligently to gather and store food for the winter. Everyone knows that story. Inevitably, winter came, and the Grasshopper begged the Ant for shelter and food, only to have a finger wagged in his face, reminding him how feckless and irresponsible he had been all summer.

The only thing was, old Hamp Pike never seemed short on cash. I recall many stories exchanged between Fred Pike and my daddy about Hamp, about him drifting in and out of my dad's life when he was a child. Hamp was generous and helped his mamma when she needed and always with a lot of money. I asked my daddy once what Hamp's relationship to the family was, and I recall him scratching his chin for a good while, and finally said that he was not rightly sure, but since his name was Pike, he must have been related somehow.

Years later, I asked Fred the same question, and I recall the same discomforted reaction, and the same answer. As I have been able to figure it out, Hamp, or Hampton Pike, was on Jim Pike's side of the family, maybe a brother, which would have made him my dad's great uncle, or a son of Jimbo's, which would have made him an uncle. No one knew for sure, but from time to time, Hamp would appear in the border counties of North and South Carolina, the home districts of the sprawling Pike family. He would always seek out Frances, wherever she was, and make sure that he gave her something. People think what people think, and maybe Fred Pike knew more than he was telling.

My daddy was born in the early 1930s, at the height of the Great Depression and Hamp was a hobo, drifting from place to place along the railway routes, pausing here and there, but never working, at least not according to the stories. He was a poker player, and they say that he never played the same table twice. He was a travelling man, but different from so many others. He always had money in his pocket. They say he dressed like a hobo and lived like a hobo, but in those days of desperation and hunger, Hamp was doing just fine.

Fred Pike at home, resting in his favorite chair. The soft lamplight, the stacks of books, and the worn comfort of the recliner reflect a life lived with both grit and gentleness. Even in stillness, Fred had stories to share—gesturing with his hands, drawing others into his memories. This image captures not just a man at rest, but the quiet dignity of a life nearing its twilight, surrounded by the familiar comforts that had anchored him for decades.

According to Fred:

"They say when it happened, Hamp walked into a bar in Oklahoma and declared – 'Stock market collapsed, paper boy just said so, must have killed a lot of cattle, and maybe some folks too, 'cause the kid sounded pretty serious.'"

Then came a lot of folks trying to get into the bank, and words quickly spread that this was no stockyard fire or barn collapse, but a much bigger deal. The bank was closed, and later a lot of folk were sitting around the town, their faces frozen in shock. It took a while for it all to sink in.

OLD FRED PIKE TOLD ME THAT HAMP WAS A COMMUNIST. "'ole Hamp," He said. "He walked with a limp, on account of taking a bullet in his leg at Honea Path during some shit that happened in 1934. That was the same year your daddy and I was born. That was the year of what the newspapers called the great textile workers' strike. My family was living and working at the Chiquola Mill in Honea Path at the time, 'fore they moved up to Fingerville. It was a bad day, a real bad day."

Hamp Pike was the only family member with a Depression-era story worth telling. Hamp was not really white trash, and in a different time and place, he might have been a professional, or a businessman, the way old Fred and my daddy were. A lot of young men at that time, frustrated by the limitations of class, and the economic ruin of the Depression, were drawn to political activism and labor. Woody Guthrie is probably the most famous one among them.

As the story goes, Hamp Pike joined the Communist Party of the United States in 1920, around about the time that it was formed. I have no way to confirm if that was true or not, but my daddy told me that Hamp lied about his age to sign up for service in the Army when the call went out for men to volunteer to fight in Europe. He saw a lot of action, but survived the war, at least physically.

The American Expeditionary Force arrived in Europe in the summer of 1917, a few months before the Bolshevik Revolution. A lot of young soldiers heard the words 'Communism' and 'Marxism' for the first time and looking around them at the horror and destruction of three years of war, it was an idea that appealed to the deep thinkers among them.

Fred Pike, and my Dad, and even old Uncle Carl were all deep thinkers. It has surprised me often on this journey how many of the people afflicted by poverty in the South were thinking folk. Donald William`s people, notwithstanding the one or two obvious exceptions, strove hard to represent themselves as people of faith and respectability. Floyd McDowell learned to play the fiddle in the church orchestra, paint watercolor landscapes, and write to express the deeper sentimentality that was often thought beyond them.

Because my daddy and Fred Pike both seized the opportunity through the military to go to college, they were both able to reap the rewards of the boom years of post-WWII. Donald opted for college and education as a way out, because that became available to more people in the 1960s and 1970s. For the likes of Hamp Pike on the other hand, those kinds of opportunities were just not available. Hamp was an intelligent, rational and thoughtful man, and a product of his age. He embraced many of the ideas and ideologies of the early twentieth century that laid the groundwork for men like my dad and Fred, and Donald and I, to achieve what we did.

Hamp was probably still a teenager when the Great War ended, and he returned to a Carolinia landscape forever altered by the industrialization of the Piedmont. He was likely reflective of a generation of people, some educated, many not, who emerged deeply scarred from that experience, and worked to salvage a better world from the ruins of war. The collapse of two of the main empires—the German and Ottoman—set the tone for the dismantling of the others—the French and the British—and the creation of the League of Nations as an early iteration of the United Nations. Mostly, though, it was the collapse of the Russian Empire, and the emergence of communism that set the tone for the great ideological contest of the twentieth century.

Hamp Pike and his brothers-in-arms found on their return from the Western Front an economic landscape now dominated by Northern capital and driven by white wage slavery. The details are all a little bit vague, and much of what I know about this story derives from eavesdropping on the yarns exchanged between my dad and Fred Pike.

The Communist Party of the United States was formed in Chicago soon after the end of WWI, with its main chapters located in the North. In the South, with the explosion of industrial labor, and the disenfranchisement of free blacks, the South should have been a natural home for labor-centric communist ideology, but it was not. As the formative black intellectual W.E.B. du Bois said to a large, mixed crowd in Columbia, SC: *This is the firing line not simply for the emancipation of the American Negro but for the emancipation of the African Negro and the Negroes of the West Indies; for the emancipation of the colored races; and for the emancipation of the white slaves of modern capitalistic monopoly.*

There have always been two sides of the socialist movement: those dedicated to labor and those to emancipation. The former tends to be working-class whites supporting organized labor, with ideologies that included the exclusion of black labor from white industries, such as the mills. And then there were others that fought racial discrimination and the slow creep of Jim Crow, and they tended to be the intellectual elites of both races. Communism in the South was deeply intertwined with the emerging civil rights movement, and would always be hostile to the white labor class, which was itself inimical to communism.

Back home from Europe, Hamp signed up as a mill worker, drifting from mill to mill, including the Chiquola Mill in Honea Path, which would be the scene of the great events on September 6, 1934. I guess he lacked the discipline and the ideological commitment to rise through the ranks of the party, and he certainly did not have the education or sophistication to become politically active in the North. His view of the social landscape was probably not much influenced by the black struggle, but by the conditions and circumstances of mill workers. Although he was never an organizer, he was in the thick of the movement which grew and fermented discontent in the ranks of mill workers across the region.

Cotton mills depended on reliable transportation, access to water, and a steady power source. As a result, they were often built where railroads and rivers converged. The Carolinas offered all three—along with vast cotton fields worked by sharecroppers and large landowners alike. These intersecting resources laid the foundation for the rise of mill hill communities that would define the Southern textile industry for generations.

'Bloody Thursday', September 6, 1934 found him on the picket lines outside the Chiquola Mill on what would be the defining moment of the great strike of that year. Hamp was probably in his thirties about then, and I doubt if he was among the professional agitators who stoked up feelings as the picket lines held, and strike breakers rushed the gate. They didn't know that Dan Beacham, mayor of Honea Path, had ordered out an armed posse of strikebreakers. There was a lot of violence, a lot of fists and clubs, but when gunfire finally broke out, six men died, and a lot of men were hit. Hamp never said nothing about that to anyone, at least according to Fred, but he walked with a limp, and sometimes a cane when the weather was cold and damp.

In any case, for a few weeks, the strike held, but in the end, desperation drove many back to the mills, and a general collapse of organization and material relief for striking workers quickly brought it to an end. I guess the great tragedy of that time is that the mills refused to take back anyone involved in the strike. Hamp, along with many others, was blacklisted, and he joined up with the Dust Bowl refugees riding the trains and making his way to California. He did not stay out West for long, and eventually he drifted back. Before long he became a periodic fixture around Fingerville and Inman, showing up from time to time, making sure that my daddy and his mama had money when they needed it.

Hamp disappeared one day, sometime in the late 1960s, maybe early 1970s, and no one heard nothing from him ever again. One night, Fred mentioned that he had heard from someone who had heard from someone else that old Hamp, probably an elderly man by then, had died of a heart attack around a poker table. It happened, as the story goes, as he was leaning across the table to scoop up his winnings, and those banknotes that he won were stuffed in his jacket pocket and buried with him the next day, somewhere, they say, in the Midwest. Ever since then, there has been a rumor in the family that Hamp had a million dollars buried somewhere or stuffed in a mattress in some old house someplace, and I reckon that is probably true.

Either way, he was never seen in Henderson County ever again.

HENDERSONVILLE IS AN INTERESTING CITY. Although Hendersonville, or what would eventually become Henderson County, attracted a few immigrants during the colonial period, it was difficult to access because it was so remote, but also because it was still Indian country. In 1785, the Hopewell Treaty was signed between the United States and the Cherokee Nation that demarcated land boundaries and opened the region for settlement. Most of the early settlers were veterans of the American Revolution who received land grants to encourage settlement, and a few who came from adjoining areas in both North and South Carolina.

The newcomers encountered a landscape defined by wide river valleys formed by the French Broad River and its myriad tributaries. Henderson County lies at the southeastern edge of the North Carolina Blue Ridge Mountains, and at its central precinct, at an elevation of about 2,200 feet, it is home to one of the broadest valleys in western North Carolina. It was an attractive country, with a salutary climate and fertile conditions. The absence of navigable waterways, however, and the poor state of overland routes tended to restrict long-distance trade and population growth.

Things changed significantly after 1827 when the Buncombe Turnpike was opened, which established Henderson County as the southern gateway to the Blue Ridge Mountains. What it mostly did, though, was open the higher reaches to wealthy planters who found refuge from the summer heat of the lowlands. This established the region as a tourist destination, which in turn gave it a cosmopolitan flavor that most other settlements in Piedmont did not reflect. One of the signature estates is the famous Biltmore, in Asheville, just a few miles from Hendersonville. The Biltmore Mansion is a stately home in the French revivalist style, built for George Washington Vanderbilt II between 1889 and 1895.

The first plat of Hendersonville was mapped out in 1844, and from the get-go, it was a wealthy center of local tourism and home of the professional classes. It was established to serve a burgeoning agriculture industry and the influx of wealthy summer-home owners. With all of that wealth, and against a backdrop of the Carolina hill country, the surroundings became attractive for the establishment of private schools and colleges, and before long, Greek revival campuses on acres of green lawns became another aspect of the general development of Hendersonville.

All of this was interrupted by the Civil War, but when the railway came, hotels and fine boarding houses lined Main Street. East of Main Street, small warehouses, factories, and workers' housing clustered around the tracks reflecting Hendersonville's position as the main railroad center in the county. By the turn of the twentieth century, there were lumber companies, sawmills, wholesale grocery establishments, two casket factories, a creamery, a wagon shop, an ice factory, and a grist mill, all located along streets oriented to the railroad. In 1913, the Freeze-Bacon Hosiery Corporation was established, with a plant on Whitted Street at Lenox Park. On the eve of World War I, Captain James P. Grey and his son founded the Grey Hosiery Mill in a one-story brick factory at the corner of Fourth Avenue East and Grove Street. At about this same time, Philadelphians George A. Moland and Bruce Drysdal established a large brick works in nearby Etowah.

So, in 1916, when Nick Wright returned home from the Great War, Hendersonville was a wealthy town of varied industry, with a vibrant working population of wage-earning whites, a somewhat smaller population of blacks, and a fast-diminishing population of sandhillers and dirt-eaters.

Nick Wright was born around 1900, or maybe late in the last decade of the nineteenth century; there is no traceable birth or death certificate. His family tree is completely obscure, with no record of where he was born, who he was born to, and who his siblings were. He appears only as Frances Margie Pike's non-surviving spouse on her death certificate, signed on 12 October 1973, and on the birth certificates of his children. He is named only as Nick Wright, not Nicholas, or

Nicodemus, or anything else, just Nick. What I understand is that his family was so remotely positioned, somewhere around Hayward County, that they missed the Great Hookworm Crusade, and Nick, along with a wide extended family, probably lived with an infestation until he and a few others signed up for the military. There he would have been treated as a matter of routine, and probably it was cured. I do not know this for sure, because the stories that have been told about him over the years describe a man very much afflicted by that old 'germ of laziness'.

The Army bonus, which was the first acknowledgement of a professional army, and the first move towards the GI Bill, was paid out in 1936, and so, for a little while at least, he had money. There are no records of employment or tax payments, and only a handful of minor arrest reports for vagrancy and petty theft. He never worked, and after his discharge, and post-amputation, he went nowhere near a hospital ever again.

They say that the lintheads worked hard to get ahead, to labor, and to build a better life. That old diagnostic feature used to identify a cracker in the old days still held true. "White trash worked hard not to work." As Nancy Isenberg, the definitive white trash scholar, put it, lintheads were the worthy, hardworking poor who strove to move up the social ladder, and [white trash were] the vulgar and hopeless who were trapped on its lowest rung.[11]

Nick Wright left the military and gravitated towards the shack towns of Hendersonville because the pickings were good. Begging, stealing, and foraging kept a body alive in those days. There were plenty of working folk to keep a small, parasitic population of dirt-eaters alive. White trash worked hard not to work, and sure enough, there are no records anywhere that Nick Wright ever held down a job any place outside of the military.

---

[11] Isenberg, Nancy. White Trash: The 400-Year Untold History of Class in America (p. 255). Penguin Publishing Group. Kindle Edition.

There were a few sizable mill villages in and around Hendersonville, and they formed part of the complex system of class and caste in Southern society. A University of North Carolina study conducted after WWII identified three distinct castes in Southern society, and those were what they called "'blue bloods', 'lintheads' and 'blacks." The study resulted in a trilogy of books called *Field Studies in the Modern Culture of the South*, with individual titles named *The Millways of Kent, The Blackways of Kent* and the *Townways of Kent*. The material was prepared under the direction of John Gillin on behalf of the Institute for Research in Social Science of the University of North Carolina, Chapel Hill, and published in 1958 by University of North Carolina Press. 'Kent', in this instance, was a fictitious town wherein the findings from a few different industrial towns were combined. Unmentioned, probably because they were few in number before the depression, and so low on the social scale, were the white trash. The involuntary sterilization program was in effect at that time, and probably the real white trash were consequently disappearing fast.

The introduction to the opening chapter of *The Millways of Kent* says about as much as we need to know at this point in our story about mill life. Nothing in it is new to us, for we have told the backstory of the mills already, but just for sake of extra context, and adding some color to this narrative, I will include a short quote:

"Just as it rises above and dwarfs the mill houses, so the cotton mill dominates the lives of the mill workers. It was the mill that beckoned the workers from the soil, provided them with houses, and presented them with the all-important weekly pay envelope. It is the mill which determines their eating time, their leisure time, and to some extent their worship time. If the mill shuts down or curtails production, life in the village is at a low ebb. When mill business is good and wages are high, life in the villages is comparatively prosperous. Villagers feel dislike of the mill as a `prison` which restricts them , and at the same time they are thankful for it as the basis of livelihood. Mill children grow up in the shadow of the

mill, knowing that it is the source of their food, clothing and shelter, and realizing, subconsciously at least, that they will likely work there by the time they reach the age of seventeen or eighteen."[12]

So much for the linthead. Then there were the 'blue-bloods', the rich folks who built and lived in those classical-revival mansions in the hills surrounding the town. There was a kind of kinship between the blue-bloods and the blacks that reflected the old, antebellum attitude of wealthy whites towards blacks. By then, most blacks in and around Hendersonville worked in domestic service, and I guess there was a lingering sense among wealthy whites that blacks were still property, and so they were treated better than the lintheads, and certainly better than any white trash.

I spoke to someone about this, who was less academic in outlook, and their sense of it was this: during the era of slavery, domestic slaves tended to be regarded as second-class family members, and because they had no income, or cash, or spending power, or any power at all, they were children in the eyes of their owners. What that implied was that every aspect of the care and maintenance of slaves fell on their owners, and so they developed a paternal view of blacks in general, a sentiment that carried over into the postbellum era. Blacks, likewise, had grown accustomed to that very paternalistic relationship, and came, even after abolition, to rely on it.

Lintheads, on the other hand, were never highly regarded. I heard a story in my research, told by an elderly man, sometime early 1950s when he and his father took the family car—a Buick Roadmaster—to Western Auto, and a sales representative was heard to remark to his colleague:

"How does a linthead get to own a car like that?"

When they got back home, my friend asked his daddy: "Why did they say that?"

---

[12] Morland, John Kenneth. *The Millways of Kent.* (University of North Carolina Press, Chapel Hill, 1958) p28

His daddy got so mad that he threatened a whipping. Being spoken down to in that way was just a fact of life for those folk in those days. Indeed, the blue-bloods very often called the lintheads white niggers.

Leaning against a wall, on the far side of the street, that modern-day Ransey Sniffle, sunken-chested, anemic, pale eyes alert for a tossed-away cigarette butt, or a bag of half-eaten food thrown to the trash, could easily have been Nick Wright. He never owned a car, because he never had a need to. On his wooden leg, given him by the Army, he would have limped his way along a footpath that climbed up through the groves of mountain laurel on the side of Stoney Mountain. There, the crackers and sandhillers from the surrounding countryside built their shacks and lean-tos, dirt-eating and moonshining. At night they wandered around the town, searching through the trash cans, stealing when they could, and raising barefoot children to the same life.

THE DEPRESSION DEALT HENDERSONVILLE a particularly savage blow. All three Hendersonville banks, heavily committed to land investments, the value of which crashed with the stock market, closed on the same day. Pretty soon, tourism ground to a halt, marking the end for most of the grand hotels for which Hendersonville had become famous. On the blocks lining the west side of Main Street, hotels like the Blue Ridge Inn, the Hodgewell Hotel, the Kentucky Home, and the Park Hill Inn all shuttered their doors and were eventually demolished. The Skyland Hotel, which opened with much fanfare in the summer of 1929 and featured seventy-six rooms at its Main Street and Sixth Avenue East location, closed, having barely seen a guest. The mills scaled back their operations dramatically, the national strike took effect, and the only work available was with the Civilian Conservation Corps, which hired young men for multiple public projects throughout the Depression.

They say, although I was never able to confirm it, that Nick Wright was part of the Bonus Army that camped out in Washington, DC, at a shack town known as Hooverville, and he was among those cleared away by soldiers using guns and tanks in one of the most despicable episodes in US history. Maybe he was. Maybe he had the gumption to get up and ride a freight train to DC. Maybe he did, but I doubt it.

Frances Pike, meantime, was born in 1918, so she was eleven years old when the Depression began, and just sixteen when my daddy was born. The birth was recorded, but no name was given for the father. She delivered in a lean-to shack with a dirt floor lent to her by a black sharecropper outside of Inman. The baby was brought into the world by a black woman, who delivered most of the babies thereabouts. No money exchanged hands, but a bucket of corn from the sharecroppers' shed. She had no contact with her family—maybe because she was a lesbian. Raping sons and daughters, it seemed, passed unchallenged before the eyes of the Lord, but never could they let such a vile secret as that see the light of day.

For a decade, my daddy and his mama moved around the border counties of the Carolinas, roaming a landscape of shuttered factories, destitute farms, and impoverished communities. Folks who were already poor were plunged into a state of destitution that was medieval in scope and severity. They gathered in shack towns and camps, in railway yards, abandoned factory buildings, and out in the open on the sides of the highways. Rickety-boned, potbellied children, most with pellagra mothers rake thin, old beyond their years, their young faces etched with worry, their eyes dead to the suffering around them.

A lot of women in those days turned to prostitution, most part-time, some in brothels, some out on the road, and some working the mill villages and camps. Frances was just a teenager, a single mother, inexplicably estranged from her family, and alone in the world. When the wind blew her into Hendersonville, on the eve of WWII, it was too late for her to rise on the tide of recovery. She threw her lot in with that sunken-chested, chain-smoking white trash with a wooden leg, living like an animal in a shack on the side of Stoney Mountain.

White Trash to Trailer Trash

*These people are pitiful. The adults are usually illiterate,
the children ragged, undernourished, disease-ridden.
Talking to these people was the most difficult assignment I had.
They are as shy as wild animals, suspicious and unfriendly
even with their neighbors in a trailer or tent six feet away.
They refuse to move into the housing projects,
partly because they are afraid of cleanliness but mainly
because they fear `the law` as they put it,
the restraint of being members of a decent community.*
Agnes Elizabeth Ernst Meyer

ON ANY OFF-THE-FREEWAY ROAD TRIP one might take around the South, a traveler is likely to see a lot of old shacks in the countryside that are collapsing in on themselves, left to rot, remnants of history. A few of them have been preserved for posterity, like, for example, the homes into which the likes of Johnny Cash, Dolly Parton and Elvis Presley were born, but most are set to disappear. On those journeys of reflection that my daddy and I took in the old days, so he could remind us both where he came from, there were no shacks in the old sense of the word, just broken-down RVs and trailers.

Of the reading material I covered getting prepped for this project, I came across a fascinating book, written by Agnes Elizabeth Meyer, described by the Encyclopedia Britannia as an 'American journalist, philanthropist, civil rights activist, and art patron'. The book was entitled *Journey Through Chaos*, and it is really a must-read for anyone interested in this general subject. The book is basically a series of articles written from the 'home front' during, and immediately after WWII. Examining several American cities, Agnes Meyer attempted to shine a light on the growing trailer culture that was emerging from the military use of trailers as emergency accommodation for soldiers, sailors and general defense workers. Some of her descriptions mirror very closely the themes we have discussed so far, but standing at the point when white trash, or impoverished Americans, began to adopt the trailer as an alternative to both the original shacks of old, and the homemade 'shanties on wheels' that carried the dust-bowlers, of Oakies, west in the direction of California.

As we have heard many times already, there is a particular sting in the term 'white trash', one that is usually intended not only to insult, but also to define; a slur not just of poverty, but of identity. It slices through class, culture, and history, attempting to reduce a whole group of people to something disposable. In the American lexicon, few terms carry as much venomous baggage as white trash. 'Trailer trash', however, its younger cousin, emerged with a sharper focus, targeting a newer subset of the same demographic, but with a modern twist.

Peter, my research assistant, who is from South Africa, told me a story that cuts to the very core of the American dilemma. Travelling through southern Africa, he and his wife, who is American, found all the hotels in the town they were visiting full. The only option was a campsite that offered trailer accommodation, or 'caravan', as they say over there. His wife refused to sleep in a trailer, to the extent that they drove on to the next town in search of something else. Her instinctive revulsion at the notion of spending a night in a trailer is a class distinction that he had no idea existed, but which she, as a well-bred, educated, and wealthy American, felt to the very core of her being.

The trailer really is a powerful symbol in the United States. On the one hand, it speaks of the open road and the magnificent highway system that we have in this country, which offers limitless scope to the overland traveler; but at the same time, it speaks of the dystopian stagnation of marginalized and impoverished communities.

Half-brothers, Vick Wright (left) and Dennis Pike (right) came together for this photograph later in life. Though Dennis had long-held differences with Vick's father, Nick Wright, time and perspective softened the divides of the past. This moment captures more than just two men standing side by side—it reflects the enduring pull of family ties and the quiet reconciliation that can come with age.

The progenitor of the modern travel trailer was the homemade shacks on wheels that the Dust Bowl refugees built on their Ford Model As, as they followed Route 66 to California. World War II introduced something more akin to the trailer that we recognize today. As many as thirty thousand trailers were used during the War as temporary housing, and because military and defense facilities were widely dispersed throughout the country, trailer communities appeared everywhere. Again, if anyone is interested in getting into that subject, Agnes Meyers' *Journey Through Chaos* is a very worthwhile resource. It is also probably worth noting that her most harrowing accounts were those written about the emerging trailer communities of the deep South.

The caste of trailer dwellers established itself mainly because the settlements were established to house the lowest level of labor in the armaments and shipbuilding industries. Somewhat like the textile mills, it was the promise of steady pay that attracted folk off the land and into urban areas. They were often the usual class of the illiterate and amoral that shocked the gentle folk of suburban communities, and this in turn led to a lot of the stigmatization and isolation that would characterize trailer parks in the future. These were, as Agnes Meyer remarked, the 'subnormal swamp and mountain folk' who set up camp in places as far removed from one another as Pascagoula and Seattle.[13]

It was not until after the War, once the defense housing aspect of trailer dwelling had diminished, that the remaining residue was seen to be mostly white trash, availing themselves of the cheapest possible housing. It is probably worth noting again that these trailer settlements were for the lowest grade of servicemen who in those days were pretty low. Whorehouses on wheels migrated between settlements along with moonshining and took on shades of the old holler and the sandhills.

Not difficult to imagine then, a modern manifestation of white trash appearing in sterile corners of big cities. Most of the trailers sold in the country through to the 1960s were consigned to the thirteen

---

[13] Meyer, Agnes Elizabeth. *Journey Through Chaos.* (Harcourt, Brace and Company, New York, 1944) p216

Appalachian states. Trailer settlements developed a reputation for vice and degeneracy, and many a blueblood youth was caught with his pants down in a trailer park on the edge of town. Media saw the lurid value in it, and an entire genre of pulp fiction dwelt on the myth and reality of the trailer park.

A more complex reckoning occurred parallel to the civil rights movement, with books and movies like *To Kill a Mockingbird*, exploring themes, not only of white trash, but racism and mental illness. The blind prejudice and familial violence that lay at the core of that story are very familiar themes to us by now.

Then came a generation that sentimentalized the old holler and the sandhills. Elvis led the pack, the son of a sharecropper, born in a shotgun shack in Tupelo, Mississippi. His self-declaration ran along the lines of – "I`m a self-confessed raw country boy and guitar-playing fool." The name 'country boy' was probably coded language at that time for white trash. Poor Southern whites seldom used the term 'white trash'. While hillbilly and redneck were more common, white trash was something rarely used by those who were so described by others, unless it was to enhance the profile of a country music singer claiming dirt-poor roots, or a company CEO trying to tell the world how far he had come. Maybe my daddy was one of those, although he sure hated that term.

Dolly Parton was maybe one of those country singers. Like Elvis, she was born a sharecropper's daughter in rural Tennessee, and it was she who famously remarked that "…it costs a lot of money to look this cheap". Johnny Cash was another, the son of a landless cotton farmer from Arkansas.[14] Willie Nelson, yet another, was born into deep poverty during the height of the Great Depression. So was Waylon Jennings, and the list goes on, not forgetting, of course, Loretta Lynn, the Coal Miner`s Daughter.

What the world owes to those folk was the creation of an artistic genre, and what would in time become a standard pillar of popular

---

[14] Johnny Cash's father was the beneficiary of a government land program that did eventually see him owning land.

culture. Country singer Steve Earl's lamentation that the army "draft white trash first around here anyway" echoes John Fogerty's plea that "I ain't no fortunate son." Neither of those two men, however, were born into poverty, at least not as Elvis, Dolly or Johnny Cash would have understood it, so their reflection of white trash values has always been performative, marking the moment that such a thing became desirable, artistically at least.

Then came the 'hick sitcom'. Three of the most popular shows in the 1960s were *The Andy Griffith Show; Gomer Pyle, U.S.M.C.,* and *The Beverly Hillbillies.* This marked, on some level at least, the rehabilitation of white trash. As I have heard a few people remark, the *Andy Griffiths Show* had more a flavor about it of the Depression era than the 1960s. The *Beverly Hillbillies* was the first to sanitize the deepest of deep Southern hillbillies. The opening pilot showed the shack and the outhouse and the almost-complete estrangement from modernity that totally satisfied the popular image of an Appalachian holler-dweller. And yet, Jed Clampett and his brood oozed the charm of innocence and simplicity, starkly contrasted against the aggressive materialism of Milton Drysdale, the urbane indulgence of Miss Hathaway, and the shallow social consciousness of Mrs. Drysdale. The absurdity of the situation was amusing in and of itself, but the relatability of Granny, with her folksy world view; of Jed, the phlegmatic country philosopher, and of Ellie May and Jethro, both irrepressibly joyous in their complete lack of understanding of the world, made them all lovable. From a subsequent generation would come *Honey Boo-boo, Duck Dynasty, Joe Dirt,* and even the Tammy and Jim Bakker phenomenon, putting modern white trash culture on display in all of its gaudy unsophistication.

But there was another side to it, too, reflected in many films and books, perhaps the most iconic of which was *Deliverance.* Anyone who has not seen or read *Deliverance* is missing one of the essential links in the chain of popular representation of white trash. The book, written by James Dickey, was published in 1970, and the movie followed a couple of years later. The story tracks four Atlanta businessmen as they embark on a weekend canoeing trip down the fictitious Cahulawassee River, which was soon to be dammed and flooded.

There are numerous themes and sub-themes in the movie, dealing with survival, masculinity and the cultural stagnation of the residents of whatever remote community James Dickey was trying to represent. One of the most famous scenes in the movie involved the guitar and banjo duet played by Drew Ballinger, played by Ronnie Cox, and the oddly savant-like, inbred boy Lonnie. That scene set the tone for the predictable cultural dissonance between a group of urban Atlantans and a community of hillbillies, who were divided by very little physical distance, but eons of cultural separation. The climactic scene took place in the woods as the friends encounter a pair of mountain men, and the character Bobby Trippe, played by Ned Beatty, is famously raped, commanded as he was, to "squeal like a pig."

There was none of the engaging innocence of Jethro Bodine, of Jed Clampett, or Luke and Bo Duke, and their kissing cousin Daisy, but plenty of the raw reality of sexual deviance that has been observed since the first representation of Ransey Sniffle.

Finally, the last chapter in the rehabilitation of white trash was the transition of prohibition-era moonshine runs into what is today the multimillion-dollar sport of NASCAR. As we all know, in 1920, the Eighteenth Amendment to the U.S. Constitution introduced Prohibition, outlawing the manufacture, sale, and transportation of alcoholic beverages countrywide. Demand for alcohol did not disappear but simply went underground. In rural areas, particularly in the Appalachian Mountains of the South, families began distilling their own liquor, commonly referred to as 'moonshine.'

The transportation of moonshine to cities and towns demanded stealth, speed, and agility. The backroads of Appalachia were often unpaved, winding, and remote, and although perfect for avoiding the authorities, they were dangerous to navigate at high speeds. To get the jump on the law, moonshiners had to modify their vehicles to go faster, handle better, and carry more product—all while maintaining a relatively stock appearance to avoid suspicion.

The drivers became local legends, celebrated not just for their mechanical skill, but for their guts and prowess behind the wheel. They often drove at night without headlights, relying on moonlight—hence the term 'moonshiner.' With the end of Prohibition, demand for moonshine diminished, and many of the former runners found themselves with fast cars and exceptional driving skills, but no outlet to use them legally. That's when the concept of informal races began to take shape. The idea of stock car racing—using 'stock' vehicles instead of purpose-built race cars—was appealing to fans. Stock cars resembled the vehicles people drove every day, creating a strong connection between the racers and the audience—and the rest is history.

It was country rock singer and songwriter Steve Earl wrote the quintessential moonshiners ballad, *Copperhead Road*, whose hero, John Lee Pettimore, comes from a family of moonshiners.

> *I volunteered for the Army on my birthday*
> *They draft the white trash first 'round here, anyway*
> *I done two tours of duty in Vietnam*
> *I came home with a brand-new plan*
> *I take the seed from Colombia and Mexico*
> *I just plant it up a holler down Copperhead Road.*

What this song describes is the transition from moonshine to marijuana, with all the same skills and methods of the old moonshiners. Meth amphetamine labs followed, and in time, fentanyl became both the drug of choice, and the main currency of illicit drug deals. My journey around Hendersonville with Lonnie McLane was punctuated with his observations of who dealt what, and where, with instructions to "Hurry the fuck up Jason. If those fuckers see me, they'll think I'm bringing the law on them, and that won't go good for me!"

THE WINDING ROAD

LEAVING DONALD WILLIAMS' HOME, WE GOT BACK on the freeway and headed back to Hendersonville. In the period since leaving, three days earlier, I had received numerous text messages from Lonnie asking for money. First, it was because he had been hospitalized for some unclear heart condition, and had only a short while to live, and then it was because of a tooth that needed pulling, and so it went on. We arrived at the house unannounced and saw Lonnie standing in the front yard while his elderly dog took a dump. Far from dying, he looked as robust and menacing as ever. Peter pointed out, though, because Lonnie was wearing a pair of shorts, that he had livid discoloration around his ankles, a pretty sure sign of circulation issues. We shook hands, his pleasure at seeing us sincere, and showing no signs of sheepishness at being caught briefly leaving his deathbed. In fact, as we walked through the door, his comment was:

"You got that Turkey 101?"

"Sure do."

"Roger that, Capt`n." He replied, grinning. "Gotta take care of a little business first."

He led the way through the kitchen. Uncle Carl was sitting at his customary seat at the kitchen table with a cup of coffee.

"Jason!" He exclaimed, his blue eyes shining, and his face cracked in a wide and toothless grin. He was dressed in an old, wash-worn t-shirt, a pair of camouflage-pattern pajama bottoms, and slippers. Standing up, we shook hands, and he offered me a seat.

"No time," Lonnie said. "Jason, you gotta help me, son."

Peter stayed in the kitchen to chat with Uncle Carl while I stepped out through the open French door with Lonnie. Outside, in an improvised pen, were two pigs, both males.

"You grab one and I'll grab the other." He said, and manhandling a damn pig, squirming and squealing like a sonofabitch, he made his way towards the road. "Jesus Christ!" he laughed, turning to look at me, "You scared of a damned pig?"

My pig was a bit less rowdy, and holding it as best I could, I followed him around to the front yard and out onto the road. We didn't have to walk far, just to the neighbor a few houses up the road. There, a pickup with its tailgate down was waiting, and an old man who looked a bit like Lonnie was leaning against.

"Morning Turd." Said Lonnie.

"Morning." Came the reply.

"This is Turd." Said Lonnie to me. I dropped my pig into the flatbed and shook hands with Turd. He was a tall, angular man of sixty or so, florid, unshaven, and with a mop of unbarbered salt and pepper hair.

"You like mountain oysters?" he asked.

"Sure do." I replied.

"Gonna be four of those dang things come dinner time."

Mountain oysters are fried pigs' balls, or any balls, really, even dogs' balls sometimes. They are an old-time delicacy for mountain folk. I recall my daddy would sometimes go down to the butcher shop and buy a mess of them, for old time's sake, and cook them up when my Mama was away. He liked them breaded and deep-fried. My mama was high-class. She'd throw a damn fit if she knew. Back in the day, poor folk went to the butcher and bought the offal and the testicles of bulls and boars, and that was damn good chow to those folks who were used to it.

"Go on." Lonnie laughed. "I know yer itchin` to ask. How'd a boy end up with a name like Turd?"

Turd chuckled.

"Tell him, Turd. This dumb prick is lookin` for stories, so give him one."

"Well." Said Turd. "I was born the third son to Lonny and Daisy McAllister, back in 1950, in a shack just up there on `ole Stoney Mountain Road. I set that place on fire a few years ago. No need to keep that kind of memory standing.

"My daddy thought naming the kids was his job, since Mama did all the hard work bringing us into the world. Said naming was the one thing he had left to do.

"When it came time for me, he couldn't think of nuthin`. He looked at me and said, 'Hell, he's the third boy, so I'll call him III.'

"That is the Roman number three." He added, just in case I did not know. "And so that's my goddamned legal name. III McAllister."

His eyes twinkled as he spoke, his delivery deadpan, and although he barely smiled, his expression was alive with the humor of it. It surely was a well-told story.

He went on.

"My brothers, meantime, heard 'Third,' and it got twisted into 'Turd', and so it stuck, for my whole life. Even my teachers called me Turd. I'm fine with it. People might call me a piece of shit, but I'm proof of life. I did two tours in Nam, and if a man can survive Nam with a name like Turd, he ain't afraid of nothin'"

He laughed, a rattling, long-time smokers' laugh, like Lonnie, and he pounded his chest with his fist.

"You step on me," he said, "and that smell's gonna follow you for a long time. So be careful."

"Turd was a linthead." Lonnie added. "Tell Jason about your lintheading, dunno why, but he's interested in that shit."

"Weren't no linthead." Said Turd. "Like a lotta kids in my time, I dropped out after tenth grade, started working in the mill. But I weren't no linthead. I was a seamster, sewing zippers into jackets for city folks that looked nothing like me. Got good at it too. Eventually made shift fixer—means I could fix the machines when they broke down. That's when things got interesting."

He leaned in a little, but spoke louder, as if he were still in the mill. It seems he was a talkative sonofabitch.

"Most of the workers were women." He said, an impious look enlivening his tired old eyes. "You learn what *they* want pretty fast."

He chuckled. Lonnie was grinning, enjoying the turn of the conversation. Those folks loved to talk about who they fucked and how they fucked them. I was beginning to get used to it by then. Those boys, and I guess the women too, love to talk about sex.

"At first," he went on. "I was just selfish, didn't know women could enjoy it too. Then I met Mabel right there." Mabel was standing on the porch smoking a cigarette, watching us. She was a standard pattern white trash woman with heavy pendulous breasts and likely much younger than him but it was hard to tell for sure.

"She taught me how to be a lover. I pleased her, and then I pleased a lot of others."

Mabel hawked and spat, flicked her cigarette butt into the road, and then turned and heaved herself back in through the screen door.

"Led to fights. Jealous husbands. Busted-up marriages. People say I've got kids all over, but I don't care. If I didn't raise 'em, they ain't mine."

Then his tone grew conspiratorial, and he lowered his voice.

"You want to know who I am now?" He looked up to make sure Mabel was out of earshot. "I crossed a line a few years back. Done a black girl. Not dark-dark. Not a full-blood black. Probably part Cherokee, what we call Red-Bone. Changed my life. She didn't want commitment—just fun. But eventually we were talking marriage."

He went silent a moment as he thoughtfully packed a dip in his cheek.

"I loved her." He said. "Thought she was pregnant a few times. We talked about what we'd do if we had a mixed baby. Then one day, she was gone."

For a moment, that crude, licentious expression was gone, and his face dropped.

"Drunk teenager ran a stop sign. T-boned her. She died on the spot. Didn't go to the funeral.. Never visited the grave. In my head, she just left. I didn't want people to know I'd loved a Black woman.

"So, who am I now? Well, just `ole Turd. That's me. Need a blue pill to get hard these days. My life's screwed. But I'll be fine."

"Got any of that shine?" Lonnie asked, breaking the tension.

"Surely do. Cliff and Skunk came by yesterday. That shit those boys cook`ll turn you blind son. Y'all want some?"

He reached behind the bench seat of his pickup and pulled out a jar. We all took a hit. Then he gave us both a quart jar for the road, and glancing at the two pigs, said something like:

"Well, fellas, I guess your time has come."

As we walked back towards the house, Lonnie said,

"I'm hungry. Shine makes me hungrier than weed." He looked at me and grinned. "Gettin` yer education started early today."

Author Jason Pike standing by the road sign marking Fingerville, the small mill town where he spent most of his youth. Fingerville was once home to a thriving cotton mill community, where generations of families lived and worked. Like many Southern mill towns, it shaped the rhythms of daily life—offering work, housing, and a close-knit sense of community, while also reflecting the struggles and hardships of labor in the textile South.

BACK IN THE HOUSE, PETER AND UNCLE CARL WERE CHATTING. Uncle Carl had a whole bunch of books out on the kitchen table, and with a long finger, was stabbing at a passage, or picture, or some damn thing, leaning forward, his eyes bright and animated. Lonnie opened the fridge and took out a piece of cold chicken.

"Time to hit the road, son." He said, and Peter rose, and after shaking Ralph's hand, followed us out the door. That tallow-complexioned girl, whoever the hell she was, was still sitting on the sofa with a kid beside her, watching TV and smoking a cigarette.

"Where we headed?"

"We gon` track down `ole Aunt Betty."

"Who's Aunt Betty?"

"Aunt Betty jus` Aunt Betty. She can tell you how and why-for.'

"Alright."

"Take a left there on Cherokee Creek Road."

Peter had his camera out, and Lonnie gave him a look.

"Careful with that thing. Folks out here don't trust nobody, `specially not some faggoty out-of-towner with a fancy talkin` accent takin' pictures an` all."

"Faggoty?" laughed Peter. "If love be love, then what of it? Methinks thou protest too much, good cousin."

"Fuck you!" Lonnie replied.

The road followed Cherokee Creek for a little while, until two lanes became one, and then the blacktop became dirt. On either side, the woods crowded in, with a trailer or a shack in a clearing from time to time, surrounded by trash and rusted cars. It was like a set for a goddamned horror movie—and that would not be the last time I thought that on that day. Although Peter had seen a bit by then, this was getting right under the skin. About a five-minute drive up a steep, rutted incline; we came to a cattle guard gate stretched across a pasture. Barbed wire ran out in both directions, rusted tight to the posts. We eased through the gate and down a dirt path that curved through a field scattered with cows and a few pigs. They all turned to watch as we passed.

"Guess this is where you got the pigs?"

"Guess so."

Then, as we mounted a rise and dropped into a holler, the house came into view.

"Christ!" Said Peter

"Damned straight," Lonnie replied with a chuckle.

A snapshot of the Pike family in the mid-1970s. From left: Dennis Pike, the eldest brother; Bethann Pike, the youngest, standing shyly in front; Jason Pike, on the right; and their mother, Nancy Pike, in the back. The clothing, hairstyles, and even the stiff posture tell the story of a Southern family making do in modest times—where Sunday dresses and patterned shirts stood in for fashion, and photographs like this became treasured family records. Beneath the simple image lies a story of resilience, family ties, and the everyday struggles that shaped Jason's early years.

The place looked like some forgotten relic from another century. One time it had been painted, but that was for sure a long damn time ago. It was one of them old shotgun shacks, from before the days of singlewides and trailers, crowded in by brush and trees, and where there was a kind of yard, it was tore up by livestock and covered in shit. One thing I noticed was no plastic trash or old cans. It seemed like maybe whoever lived in this house had not yet arrived in the twenty-first century. As we drew up, an old hound dog raised himself off the porch and bayed long and laboriously. That triggered an eruption of smaller dogs that tumbled in a noisy pack out of the open front door. It truly was like a goddamned movie.

A face appeared at the door, and out stepped a short, stooping, elderly woman with a face as ruddy and coarse as old leather. In her hand was a double-barrel shotgun, and I swear she looked like she could have been Granny Clampett, except she was wearing a soiled t-shirt and the usual Walmart pajama bottoms. It was like a uniform in those parts. Lonnie hopped out of the car fast, probably trying to head off any trouble.

This photograph shows Gertie Goode (1877–1970), Donald's great-grandmother, who was born in the American South during the Reconstruction era. Known within the family for her stern presence, she occasionally cared for young Donald during his childhood. Family stories recall that she had a habit of giving him the "evil eye" and playfully pretending to cast hexes—gestures that left a lasting impression on him and contributed to her reputation as both a caretaker and a figure of quiet intimidation.

"Good morning, Aunt Betty," He said, real polite.

Betty squinted hard at him. "What chu want Lonnie, you fuckin` piece of shit? I outa shoot yer fuckin` ass right now. Where my money? Y'all took two fuckin` boar and you ain't paid me shit."

"Well, this here is my cousin Jason, and he gonna pay you right now."

"He looks like the law." She said, narrowing her eyes to look at me.

"He's Army."

"Army?"

"Yes Ma`am!" Said I.

"Well, hell, why didn't you say so."

She lowered the shotgun and placed it out of sight in the doorway.

"Two hundred and seventy-five dollars." She said, holding out her hand.

"Better give it to her." Said Lonnie. I had plenty that I wanted to say about it but right then was not the moment. I took out my billfold and gave her three one-hundred-dollar bills.

"Ain't got no change." She said.

"Keep it." and with that, the tension was broken.

"Well, hell!" She said, "I got twenty-five dollars of shine somewhere."

"Bring it out." Said Lonnie. He took out a pack of cigarettes and offered one to Betty.

"Don't mind if I do."

She regarded me thoughtfully as she puffed on her cigarette. It was hard to tell how old she might be, but was surely real old.

"You, Dennis' boy?" She asked.

"Sure am." Said I.

She turned to Lonnie.

"You're a worthless fuck, and there's a whole lotta lazy in you, but I don't meet strangers, and I believe in entertaining angels unaware. So y'all welcome."

Peter was introduced, and, arching her eyebrows at his impeccable British manners and accent, she said, "Sure is fancy."

Lonnie, meantime, climbed onto the porch and shouted into the dim interior, "Y'all home, motherfuckers?"

Betty scowled. "Where the fuck else would they be?"

She turned and hollered into the house:

"Hey y'all, get your asses out here—we got company!"

Four adults shuffled out onto the porch. Two of them had Down syndrome, and one was a midget. The last was a wiry, misshapen man who said not a single word—just kept coughing, hacking up phlegm, and spitting it off the porch, regular, like a metronome. They all stood around on the porch just staring. It was very off-putting. Betty ordered the older man, the hacking-cougher, to bring out a jar, and silently, he walked back into the house. We arranged ourselves on the porch steps.

"Jason's writing a book or some damn thing," Lonnie explained. "Wanted to meet up with some of the family, so I figured we'd start with you."

Betty smiled—not sweet, but honest—and launched right into her story like she'd been waiting on someone to ask.

"Well." She said. "I was born Betty James, Married my cousin Rudy Wright when I was fifteen. That was normal back then. 'Cept me and Rudy were double first cousins. Might've been too close—like lettin' dogs from the same litter breed. You get fucked up puppies."

She inclined her head as she said it, back to the mute assembly of souls behind her. None said a word, or altered their expressions, or even seemed to be aware that we were strangers.

The older man stepped out of the house with a jar half full, and it was handed around. She cocked her head towards him.

"My firstborn. That's Timmy-boy. He's got 'im-fa-seem-ma' and 'diver-tick-you-lie-to-us.' Means he can't breathe, and his guts is stucked together. I reckon it's 'cause Rudy had him smokin' by age five. By ten, he was on three packs a day, still does. School kept suspending him for smokin' in the bathroom, so we just pulled him out. Probably stunted his growth."

She paused for a long hit from the jar before she continued. Timmy-boy pointed at Lonnie's pack of cigarettes, but Lonnie ignored him. He was pretty tight with his cigarettes.

"Timmy-boy always wanted to be a wrestler. Watched it on the TV Rudy stole from some house over near Rutherfordton when the REA brought electric out here. I'd return that TV if I knew where it came from, plus it's busted now. Timmy-boy was glued to that damned thing. Rudy found out there was a local bout at the high school and took him to try out. We didn't know it was sometimes fake. They put Timmy-boy in the ring for a gag during the show—they beat the shit outta him. It was a cryin' shame. Really beat the shit out of him, like throwing a chihuahua into the ring with a fighting pit bull. They thought it was funny, but it was real bad. Real bad. He never wanted to wrestle again. Sometimes I think that beatin' what tore his insides up."

With a softer expression on her face, Betty nodded toward one of the women.

"Next was Polly. We knew something was off—she never crawled or walked before she was three."

Peter later described Polly as revolting, and she kinda was. She had real bad periodontitis, the scars of old acne, and her hair was hacked short. You could see how bad her teeth were because her nostrils were jammed up with snot, like a baby, and so she was breathing out of her mouth. She was looking intently at me, through pale blue eyes, the only attractive thing about her, and I had the horrible thought that she was going to try and get fresh with me.

"Doctors said she was a 'mon-ga-loid.'" Betty went on. "Couldn't talk then, and hardly talks now. Government folks came by to try and teach her, but she never learned much. She can sweep a floor, though."

She pointed at another. "Then came Annette."

I glanced at Annette and shuddered.

"Same again, but she talks some. She can sing too—real nice. She just listens to songs on the radio and sings 'em right back. We gave her a radio for Christmas one year and she still listens to the damn thing. Sings all day long.

"Rudy dropped dead one day—came in from workin' cows, sat down in the kitchen, had a heart attack. Timmy-boy and me buried him out back. We still get a Social Security check cause we never reported him dead. Every time a government person comes looking— they don't come often, but they come sometimes—we just say he's up the hill huntin' bear.

"Not long after, Jimmy showed up. Courted me, said he loved me. I'll say this—he was better in the sack than Rudy ever was. Did stuff I didn't even know people could do. He told me he was a virgin first time we laid down, but somebody sure trained him right."

She chuckled.

"Anyway, I got pregnant again. Had Debbie. Turns out she's got a 'hore-moan' problem. Never got over three feet tall. Never hit puberty. Just stayed like a little girl, even in the mind. Can't have kids or nothing."

She narrowed her eyes and looked at Lonnie, then at me, and then at Peter, her gaze lingering suggestively on his crotch. He squirmed a little.

"So you're probably wonderin' where Jimmy is? Well, Polly had a baby when she was fourteen. She can't talk, so we'll never know what happened. She would just say *immy*— just that—so it coulda been Timmy-boy or Jimmy. Timmy-boy swears he didn't touch her. He was old enough, that's the truth, and folk can be strange, but I believe him.

"That left only Jimmy, so I had to get rid of him. Now we get his social money. He's buried out back, too, 'side Rudy. He spends a lotta time up there in them hills hunting bear too. Wonder sometimes what the two of them talk about up there is those bear hills. Maybe regretting their sinful ways. Maybe. I sure goddamned hope so."

She motioned to Lonnie to give her a cigarette, and he did. Timmy-boy followed the exchange with hungry eyes.

"Give him a goddamned cigarette you cheap motherfucker."

Lonnie did, and with infinite gentleness, Timmy-boy took it and leaned in for a light.

"Government came and took that baby." She went on. "Never told us where. My grandbaby's out there somewhere, and I pray for her every night."

Then she shrugged.

"Prob'ly for the best

"So now it's me and these four, livin' off what the government sends us. Rudy and Jimmy's social payment, disability, food money. We make do."

She looked us over once more, then stood up and leaned on the porch railing.

"That's my story. Just survivin'."

Something told me that she was done talking. Lonnie said that we got other visits to make, and Peter asked if he could use the can before we left.

"You don't wanna do that." She chuckled. "Best piss in the yard."

The three of us walked back to the car, escorted by the hound dog. The five of them remained on the porch and watched us leave.

"Don't be strangers, y`hear!" She called after us, and we all waved. Back in the car, Lonnie reached for the bottle of Wild Turkey and took a deep hit before he offered it to me. I had a hit, and so did Peter.

"So, who was Rudy Wright?" Peter asked.

"Hell, I don't know," Lonnie replied, "one of my grandaddy's family, I guess. Maybe a cousin or a nephew. Mama thinks he was a nephew, her cousin, but she don't rightly know. I know Betty separate from any of them. She cooks and stills, and she sells pigs and cows sometimes, so I do business with her. She's a dirty bitch. I fucked her one time, and it was as loose as a noose before the drop—like tossing a fucking catfish into a bucket. Stank like a fucking skunk too."

Peter chuckled.

Author Jason Pike placed second in a watermelon-eating contest, a lighthearted competition that carried deeper roots. His father, Dennis Pike, had once taught his sons how to swipe watermelons from fields—an old Southern mischief that turned into a lifelong love of the fruit. What began as boyhood lessons in mischief became a family memory that ripened into tradition, reminding Jason of his father's influence even in unexpected moments.

BACK ONTO THE HIGHWAY, we headed north about fifteen minutes to a little wayside diner called Paul's. It was early lunchtime, and pickup trucks lined the lot, while the inside was crowded with working men in high-vis coveralls. We took a seat and ordered from the board. Lonnie was part-way drunk, loud and rumbunctious, and he made a significant point of introducing us to a couple of guys that he knew. He bragged on my rank, and that Peter was from overseas, offering demonstrative assurances that he was neither gay nor liberal, just foreign.

One of his friends was Devin. Devin was too slick to be a working man, so probably a hustler, like Lonnie, but without the hulking brutality and mangled fists. He had the furtive look—spatial awareness, they call it in the military—of a man long used to living on the fly. He joined us at our table.

"Devin just got outa the pen." said Lonnie, to which Devin nodded, as if he was admitting to nothing worse than an honorable discharge from the military. "He's my main man, ain`t `cha Devin?"

"Sure am."

"You need anything, anything son, Devin your man. Tell 'em your angle Devin."

He grinned, bearing large, nicotine-stained teeth, and two lines of missing molars.

"I don't clock in, man," he said. "I just got a real good system. I know my way around computers and phones and shit, and I figured out how to fleece rich, soft-bellied liberals from Charlotte, Atlanta, Greenville, and Asheville like it's a game.

"S`all on Facebook. I find some overpriced bullshit—cars, couches, whatever—don`t matter. I message 'em like I'm buyin`. Always offer full price so they don't get spooked. Then I spin the story. Tell `em I work search-and-rescue dogs, and I got a bitch `bout to drop a litter any minute. Say I can`t drive more`n an hour from home."

"Them commie liberal types love a dog story. Gets 'em all soft. I tell 'em to meet me at the Credit Union in Waynesville so they feel safe. Then once they show up, I backpedal—say the item ain't what it looked like in pictures or I got a sudden emergency. Offer 'em way less—sometimes half. They already drove two hours to meet me, so they cave. Don't wanna haul that shit back. Then I just sell it on to the meth cookers up there in the mountains. They got cash so they cool. Everyone happy. It's all legal. Willing buyer and willing seller, and all that shit. Ain't liftin' nothin', and jackin` nothin` and ain't hittin' no one. Just talkin'. And my old lady stays happy 'cause the bills are paid, and I ain't workin' myself into the grave."

Then he leaned in a little.

"And I get to screw over them damn Yankee liberals tryin' to turn these hills into some Whole Foods paradise. They want the Southern charm—well, I give it to 'em in the fuckin` ass! Bless their heart and fuck 'em six ways from Sunday."

From left: Dennis Pike (Jason's father), Jason Pike (center), Dennis Pike (Jason's brother, right), and Phillip Bagwell (back), the farm's owner. Not pictured but present that day was Phillip's wife, Bethann Bagwell—Jason's sister. The visit to the Bagwell farm was more than a family gathering; it was a return to roots, where the land itself carried memories of labor, kinship, and the Carolina way of life that shaped them all.

LONNIE LIFTED ANOTHER HUNDRED OFF ME FOR DEVIN. Stories ain't free, he said, or something like that. I figured there`d be a split. Lonnie was making money, and he was in buoyant humor as we wrapped up and walked back to the car. Draining the last out of the first bottle, he cracked the seal on the second and got to talking that he wanted to get high. He had money in his pocket, and when a boy like Lonnie gets money, first thing he thinks of is drugs.

We left Paul's Diner and headed west, deeper into the folds of the Carolina hills. Lonnie said there were a couple more places he wanted to swing by, but he gave a little warning too—said we going pick up some rock, so things might get strange. Knowing Lonnie like I did, that could mean anything, from a pig roast to a backwoods militia camp.

We stopped briefly at a scenic lookout. It was a lovely scene. The whole valley stretched out below us, all green pasture and slow-moving cattle, stands of mountain laurel and the blue line of Appalachia in the distance. Lonnie was drinking hard. The day had already taken a few odd turns, and likely there would be a few more, so Lonnie getting sloppy on Wild Turkey seemed like the least of it. I was probably in no shape to drive myself, but Lonnie laughed it off like it was nothing. Said driving while drinking wasn't a crime in the those parts—said it was practically a pastime.

We got back on the road and rolled along for a while before turning onto a dirt road, one of those winding, gully-cut tracks that leave the highway with no signage. Those kind of mountain roads were everywhere, snaking through old logging routes and deer paths, going who the hell knows where. The undercarriage dragged a few times over a high center ridge, and almost dipped into deep gullies on either side. It was hairy as hell. After what seemed like a ten mile ride we came to a locked gate. Lonnie pointed to a hunting cam nailed up high on a pine and said,

"That thing right there is a decoy. Real ones are buried in tree knots and fence posts—cop-proof."

Then he climbed out and weaved his way across the gravel to the gate, and then he lifted it clean off its hinges. "Old mountain trick," he said, "everybody up here knows it. Gates only keep out the honest thief."

We pulled through and Lonnie dropped the gate back on the hinges behind us.

On we rolled, tires crunching on the gravel. The track was narrower still, crowded in on both sides by trees such that there was barely any sunlight. The gloom and silence were as eerie as hell.

"Is this where we die?" Peter asked. "Is this the part where they find the car and never find us?"

Lonnie cackled with more bravado than he maybe felt.

Then, up ahead, tucked back behind a wall of brush, a sagging old single-wide trailer appeared, set in a dappled clearing, and strangely free of the kind of trash and debris you get used to when you see a singlewide in the woods. I couldn't figure how they hauled that damned thing up there. Must have been one hell of a job. Then, out of the corner of my eye, I saw a figure step out of the shadows behind us, a long gun squarely leveled at the rear glass, and the back of Peter's head.

None of us moved. Lonnie was suddenly as sober as a preacher.

"Just wait here." He said. "This is Earl, and he's my half brother. I owe him money, so he might be pissy."

He got out slow, hands up like this was something he'd done before.

"Howdy Earl." He said. The rifle was dropped.

"You fuckin` cheatin` sonofabitch."

The two men shook hands. Lonnie stood in a pool of sunshine, but Earl seemed to linger purposefully in the shadows. Although I could not get a clear look at him, what I could see was a tall, sinuous figure that reminded me instantly of the many drill sergeants I had run into during my military career. I figured that he was probably ex-military, and the way he handled that rifle told me that he sure knew his way around guns. Most mountain men did, and a lot of mountain men, and a lot of those militia guys, are ex-military.

Lonnie whistled, and waved to us to join him. Peter and I tentatively stepped out of the car into the cool, fresh mountain air, and very cautiously stood waiting as Earl stepped out of the shade and approached us. Sure enough, he was military. His back was straight, his teeth clean and well formed—the work of an Army dentist, probably—and although his black hair was uncut under a faded green John Deere baseball cap, he still looked military.

We shook hands, and his grip was firm and strong.

"You Army?" He asked, looking at me intently, through eyes overhung by heavy, knitted brows, blue, sharp and penetrating. While his attitude was friendly, he was looking at me hard, the rifle loosely cradled the way a combat soldier does, ready to bring it into action at a moment's notice. He knew his business.

"Thirty-one years."

"Infantry?"

"Medical."

He nodded.

"Welcome brother. I won't be insulting you today. You're already Army…that'd just be cruel."

He grinned. The rules of the brotherhood are strong in the South.

"You?" I asked.

"Corps."

"Muscle Always Required, Intelligence Not Essential."

He laughed.

"Fuck you!"

He waved us up onto the porch, like we were old friends, and not five minutes removed from having a rifle aimed at our heads. The porch was nothing more than a poured concrete slab out front of the trailer, but someone had made it feel comfortable and lived-in. I figured we'd probably be meeting one of those behemoth white trash women that every trailer guy seems to love, or settle for, although it did seem to me that Earl had his shit together a lot better than most of those guys.

Peter and I seated ourselves on a couple of mismatched rocking chairs between which was a cooler filled with cans of PBR. The air had that clean, mountain purity, with shafts of light cutting through the trees, and the breeze soft, fragrant and slow. Earl didn't say much at first. He rested the rifle against a grill and regarded us as he pulled a camp chair. He asked where we were coming from, made a few neutral remarks about the weather, keeping it civil, but still wary, in particular of Peter, whose cultivated airs seemed to confuse him. Not many folks like Peter ever make their way that deep into the mountains.

Then the screen door creaked and a woman stepped out. He glanced up.

"This here's Rhonda," he said.

I was taken by surprise. Rhonda was a different kind of woman for those parts. White trash women are almost always fat, you get used to that, but hillbilly women often are not. Rhonda looked like a mountain woman, barefoot, hair tied up and wearing a loose tank and daisy dukes. Her skin was leathery and tanned, her limbs like long sticks of beef jerky, and her teeth, even though they all still seemed to be in her head, were gapped and uneven. I couldn't say exactly how old she was, but she surely was older than Earl, and even though she was no beauty, she had that kind of animal sexuality that told me things could get pretty wild up there in that holler. Once she was introduced, she sat on the steps of the singlewide and lit a cigarette, watching us all with reserved interest.

As Lonnie and Earl bantered, a kind of preamble before the moonshine and methamphetamine appeared, I was struck by how similar Earl was in mannerism and speech to Ralph. It was easy to see that they were probably related. Both had the same, odd, old-English style of talking, as if they were reciting folk-poetry in simple, rhythmic stanzas. Uncle Carl was an old-timer, a master storyteller in the old, traditional style. His stories were rarely abridged, and once begun, could consume a whole evening. Earl was kind of the same. Relaxed now in his chair, a can of beer in his hand, he was rocking slightly, and speaking in precisely the same style, interrogating Peter with sincere interest.

"From South Africa? Goddamn. I was in Africa in `92, when the Corps was deployed to Somalia. Was only there for a little while, though. Fuckin` shithole."

And so it continued. By happy coincidence, Peter had written some report about Operation Ranger and the Battle of Mogadishu, so he knew a lot about it, and he and Earl quickly found common ground. It always does amaze me how, once those mountain men are done snarling and sniffing round a strangers ass, their tails get to wagging pretty quick. Lonnie told Earl that I'd pay him what he was owed, and Rhonda was ordered in to get the fixings. Soon after Earl and Lonnie were swapping a glass bowl, blowing plumes of white smoke into the clean air. Rhonda twisted the lid off a mason jar filled with shine and sat it on the table.

"See here," said Earl, slapping her ass, "I got nuthin` to say about myself, but my lady here, she got a story. She was a preacher's wife one time. Came up here from Rock Hill when I got out. He was a nice enough fella, I guess, just couldn't keep her satisfied. They say them women from Rock Hill, they got fire in their pants."

Rhonda, back on the steps, listened, her chin cupped in one hand and a cigarette in the other, a look of amiable amusement in her eyes.

"Don't matter if she did marry a man of God, she burns hot, and no Fuckin` holy water gonna put that fire out. It takes the staff of the Lord I tell ya, *the staff of the Lord!*"

"Amen." said she.

More rock was burned, and then Lonnie and Earl got up and went back of the trailer, and before long a burst of automatic gunfire, and peals of laughter, shattered the calm of the late afternoon. Rhonda scowled, stood up and screamed such that I almost jumped out of my skin.

"Goddammit Earl!"

More laughter, and then Lonnie reappeared, and motioned me to follow him. Peter and Rhonda were in conversation, and so they stayed in their seats as I got up and followed Lonnie back behind the trailer.

There was a backyard-type clearing there, with a couple of dog kennels and an old Ford F-250 pickup truck parked in the shade of a tree. I followed the two of them down a footrail that led into the deep shade of the woods. It occurred to me that there were dog kennels but no dogs, and almost as I entertained that thought, I heard the baying of a hound dog in the near distance. Our movement through the woods, as silent as it was, had alerted a dog somewhere. It was an eerie sensation, like a scene out of *Deliverance,* or some damned thing, and as we closed in on the source of the barking, another joined in, and then another.

I heard the musical notes of a mountain spring before abruptly the footpath broke out of the forest and entered into a clearing. At the edge of the clearing a tiny creek flowed between rocky banks, and tucked into an overhang was an old, broken-down structure, probably a home one time, one of those old shotgun shacks. The barking stopped, and three villainous-looking dogs, tied to a long running wire, wagged their tails frantically as Earl approached. He untethered them and they mobbed him as he pulled the door of the shack open.

I sensed that we were about to get into a working meth lab, but that was not how it was. Inside, the building was hollowed out and reinforced, the rear backing up into an excavated portion of the hillside, sectioned off with an old blue tarp. Behind the tarp there was a folding table with two butane camping stoves, and not a damned thing else. No gear, no bottles, no residue. Just damp damp-smelling space.

"This is where we cook," said Earl. "But we never leave shit up. Soon as we're done, everything gets broken down, scrubbed, packed away. Leaving it out? That's what gets you prison time son."

The military way, I thought to myself. This boy was well-trained.

Lonnie was leaning against the doorway, smoking a cigarette.

"My job is security." He said. "Me and them boys."

He pointed back at the three dogs rooting around the edges of the clearing.

"We keep watch on the road with a two-way radio while the cooking is happening."

Earl nodded.

"Our dealers give us what we need to make it, and Lonnie runs it back down when we're done. Everyone gets what they need. Rhonda and I live quiet. This ain't no kingpin setup—we just keep enough going to stay happy. It's smart. Fast in, fast out. Low labor, low risk, big enough return. This won't last forever, nothing ever does, but right now? We're good."

Before we left, Earl offered me a sample, but I declined.

"Suit yourself." He said. "Adults do adult things. They pick their poison. I ain't no one's babysitter—I'm just supplying the market."

This photograph shows a family meal around the kitchen table, set with its red-and-white checkered cloth. On the far left sits Cora Pike, who at the age of 14 married Jimbo Pike, a man more than twenty years her senior. At the table, Jason's brother rests his arm on the chair in a striped shirt, with Jason seated beside him, identifiable by his blond hair. On the far right, looking toward the camera, is Betty Pike, remembered for her distinctive manner of speaking. Next to her sits Louise Pike, between Betty and Cora. True to family tradition, biscuits and gravy accompanied nearly every meal, and a pan of biscuits sits in front of Betty—always recalled as the best the family ever tasted.

PETER, MEANTIME, STAYED BACK AT THE TRAILER, chatting to Rhonda. He kept covert recordings of everything said during these encounters, and his conversation with Rhonda was kind of interesting.

Turns out she was a mountain girl, from somewhere in Kentucky, but she was also a high school teacher with a college diploma, and I guess the kind of folk that she could have an educated conversation with were scarce thereabouts. She met Earl through the drug scene in Rock Hill, although she was married to the preacher at the time. She had never been able to carry a child to term, and she was real depressed about that. One night she went out with her girlfriends, and they got to playing pool with some local boys, and then she got to drinking with one of them—that was Earl. She liked his manliness, his simplicity and his clear moral compass. He was untroubled by so many of the complications of city life, of marriage, career and faith community, and something about him spoke to her of the life she had left behind up there in the hollers of Appalachia.

"You'll never get him to say it." She said. "And you would never guess it by lookin' at him, but he's a fuckin' millionaire. Drug business is good business, and he knows how to handle the law around here."

Kind of a different story to what Earl told us, but I get why he would be cagy about it, since the money was probably stashed in cash somewhere thereabouts.

He gave her a little rock for her depression, she said. Said it would lift her up, and it did. Pretty soon she was an addict, lost her job at the Christian school, and then one day she came up the mountain to live with Earl.

"Preacher Calvin, my ex, well he was a good man," She said. "I ain't denying that, but some people can't fill what's empty in you. Truth is, I got messed up early. My uncle, JB, started messing with me when I was just fourteen. That's the shit I don't miss about mountain life. I never told nobody. That's how it always is. Snitches get stitches. I didn't even think too. He treated me different after that—bought me things, talked nice. And I was just a kid. Maybe I thought that was love, or something like it. Hell, I don't know."

She paused, took a hit from a jar, and went on.

"Later, while I was at college, I met a soldier. Young guy from Lafayette, just back from Germany. He showed me what it could really be like—the kind of touch that ain't about taking. I still remember nights we'd sneak out back after everyone went to sleep."

The memory of it prompted her to smile.

"It didn't last though." She said. "Never does. He left. I thought maybe I was carrying his baby, but that ain't never going to happen for me. Looking back, maybe that's was a mercy."

She met Calvin at church, she said.

"Church was kinda my drug in those days. He had a decent job, a room in his parents' mill house, and he seemed steady. I thought I loved him, and we were married pretty quick. I pretended to be a virgin, never said nothing about JB or the soldier. I needn`t have bothered. He popped quicker than corn in the skillet."

She smiled.

"Then, when he decided he was called to preach, I tried to play the part. But I was just acting. I was empty inside, because I couldn't give him kids. I wasn't number one on his list—maybe not even number four. God, the church, his parents—and then me. I was pretty much alone."

Earl, she said, reminded her of that soldier, said he looked at her like she was worth saving.

"And I fell," she said. "Hard. Started with a little drink, then weed, then Earl gave me that damn rock. It got bad. I'd do anything for the next hit. Even out behind Paul's Diner in the middle of the day. I was so goddamned busy I needed a punch card and a traffic controller. I was on my knees so much I had to start wearing pants to church to cover the bruises."

A rueful smile played fleetingly across her face.

"Then he pulled me out. Got me hooked, but then got me clean. I know it don't look like much, but I'm safe now. I've got peace. And peace is enough."

BY THE TIME WE GOT BACK ON THE ROAD, Lonnie was wide-eyed and amped up, the liquor having no apparent effect, and now he was real hungry. The afternoon was slipping into twilight, and by the time we were back on the blacktop road, the headlights were on.

"You boys wanna eat?" He asked. "I'm so hungry I could eat the north end of a southbound mule."

He began stabbing at his phone, and after a few rings, it was answered.

"Aunt Mildred?"

He covered the phone and grinned at me.

"I owe her money, too."

I tried to mentally calculate how much cash I had left in my billfold. This was all getting kinda pricy.

"Got some outa town boys here want some homestyle Southern cookin'…and I'll settle up with you too."

Thus we began a twisted odyssey along a network of rural and suburban roads, with pleasant, spacious properties on either side, and occasional open stands of field and woodland. At the end of a long road, almost lost in the twilight, stood a period, single-story house, modest, but well maintained. It seemed at a glance too neat and ordered to blend with the theme of the day. The driveway was graveled, and lined with a short row of trees, and the grounds, such as I could see them, were well tended, with a mowed lawn and flower beds managed with the loving care of a devoted gardener. It was all pretty unexpected. The sound of an approaching car triggered a cacophony of barking dogs, and a porch light came on, and then a line of fairy lights in the garden illuminating a pathway. It was a bit like driving into a Thomas Kincaid painting.

The large figure of a woman appeared in the lit doorway.

"Y'all go on and get out." Said Lonnie "Ain't nothin' to worry about here."

We approached the porch a few steps behind Lonnie. He mounted the steps and he and the woman embraced briefly, exchanging fond greetings. It reminded me way more of Aunt Rita than it did of Betty, and the whole place looked conventional, respectable and almost suburban.

Lonnie introduced us.

"This here's Mildred." He said. "She's an aunt of our grandmother—the best cook in this whole dang county."

"I heard about you!" I said, shaking her hand lightly. "You were Fred Pike's sister?"

"Half-sister." She said.

"Your daddy was Will Pike, Jimbo's twin brother?"

"Sure was, Margie was my cousin by marriage, I think it was cousin, though she older 'n me by ten years or more."

"Well I be darned." I said.

Under the porch light, I could see that she was elderly, mid-eighties, maybe more, strangely similar in appearance to Aunt Rita, but thick-set and heavier. Her eyes were blue, clear and bright, and her smile showed a set of clean, oversized dentures.

"C'mon in." She said.

Inside, the hallways smelled of dogs. We were mobbed by a pack of little toy dogs that dominated the first few moments as Mildred cooed and chided until they settled down some. The walls were paneled in 1970s-style wood vinyl and were hung with random pictures and old photographs. I was surprised to see an old framed photograph on the wall that looked a whole lot like Hamp Pike. The scene was a picnic somewhere, and the tall, elegant figure of 'ole Hamp was unmistakable.

"That Hamp Pike?" I asked her, and she looked at me sharply, her eyes narrowed.

"Sure is,' she said, "he was your…"

She stopped herself, and thinking better of whatever she had a mind to say, she guided us into the living room. There, seated on a pattern sofa watching TV, was a woman of similar age, but slight, and anxious looking, reminding me of Aunt Jo-lyn. Mildred did not so much introduce her as point her out.

"That's Miss Patty," she said. "She's my sister. Don't mind if she don't say much. She listens more than she speaks."

Upon that, she turned purposefully to look up at me, her hands on her hips.

"Now, Jason." She said. "Aunt Rita called me yesterday and told me you would likely be around, and she told me to say nuthin` `bout `nuthin, so nuthin` is what I'm gonna say, just so you know."

With that, and with no further explanation, we were ushered through a doorway into the kitchen, a lovely, homely room, warm from the range and smelling richly of good food. As we took the seats offered to us at the kitchen table, Mildred bustled around. She set down a pitcher of iced tea and remarking several times that we were lucky because she cooked that day for Amos, the old black man who came by sometimes to mow the lawn.

"Country ham, greens and mash potato." She said. "Nuthin` fancy today."

I asked her about the house, and she looked around the room thoughtfully, her hands on her hips.

"Daddy built it." She said. "In bits. When I was little it was just a shack, but over the years they added and improved it. Daddy, Jack and Donny dug the well out back—we lost Donny in Vietnam, that's him there, on the wall, and Jack, well, Jack, he out on the road somewhere. Before that, we'd haul water up from a spring down the hill. Mama got tired of that and told Daddy she wanted water closer to the house, so he started digging. Took him two years to dig than dang hole down sixty feet deep, and it ain't gone dry yet. Still pulls up good, clean water.

"Then, forty years back, maybe more, Bobby Joe, he rented some land from Daddy, he was a Seabee one time, and he brought in a crew of old buddies with a rig. They drilled a proper well and plumbed the house. Got us runnin` water and even an indoor toilet."

She chuckled.

"We thought we were so dag gum fancy. Didn't know no better. Might as well have been royalty, far as we were concerned."

Lonnie guided the conversation around family, and this and that, and then he asked, kinda out of left field, if she remembered my Daddy.

"Sure, I remember Dennis." She said, with a smile. "Sure do. Best looking boy I ever seen. I guess he was my half nephew, or somethin` like that. Every girl in the county had a thing for `ole Dennis, he sure was a handsome boy. Ever`one called him 'Pic' in them days, don't rightly know why, I guess it came from 'Pike'. Just always did. I remember when he up and disappeared. Word was he just took off.

"Word was too he gave his step-daddy, `ole Nick, a beating. I kinda think Nick deserved it. There was one worthless son of a gun right there. Spent his life plaining about his dag gum disability, always beggin`, always asking, never workin`. Would come by here, sayin` his kids was starving, and Daddy would offer him work, and he would sure leave quick then. Dag gum, you'd think that rascal was the only one who ever got wounded in war. We lost Donny, like I said, but plenty others round here got messed up in that war, `n done fine after…

"Now look what I done." She said, as she arranged the food on the table, and handed out plates. "I promised Aunt Rita I'd say nuthin` and now I been runnin` my mouth off."

"Well." Said Lonnie. Jason wants to hear some damn stories. He's writing a fancy book or something. You might as well tell him now, since you started."

"No need for that kind of language Lonnie." She replied sharply. "You ain't too old for a slap upside the head!"

He laughed, and commenced heaping food on his plate. She sat down, smiling at him fondly.

"Well." She said, after a while. "Ain't much to tell, not compared to others. I had six brothers and four sisters. Just me and Patty left now in this house. Donny was the youngest, he was the one who was going places. He was a sergeant in the 101st Airborne—that's him right there in that picture—he was killed in Hue in 1968, Daddy never got over that.

"Frankie got polio when he was just a kid, walked with crutches all his life. He died under a John Deere one day when it fell on its side and trapped him under.

"Last I heard of Jack he was working in a fish cannery in Alaska, heard somewhere that he joined a monastery in Canada, someone else told me he died of AIDs in California. He was a strange boy, Jack, he was my favorite brother I guess. Pete, Stu and Roy were all military, they all retired in pretty good shape. Roy the last of them, and he died in the fall. Peaches, Sue and Lisa all married military, busy now with grandkids and stuff. Funny thing—all the boys died, but the girls are still around."

"Did you ever marry?" I asked.

"No sir. Just about every boy around these parts joined up or was drafted, and so many never came home that it left a scarcity of men to marry. Mama needed help with Miss Patty, so I stayed for that, and when Mama died, there was no one else left to take care of her. I might`a left one time. Back in fifty-four, I met a real sweet boy—he was eighteen, I was fourteen. He joined the Marines and said we'd marry when he came back from Korea. My mama, she told me to be careful, but to give him somethin' to come home to."

A rueful smile played on the corners of her mouth.

"We had a good week together. Learned a lot about life. I cried when he left. Never saw him again."

I apologized for raising it, but she waved that aside.

"It ain't a bad memory." She said. "We was all proud of him. He was buried with a medal on his chest. Life's like that, we all have two things in common—you're born, you die. What's in between is what you make of it. He had near enough nineteen good years. Got to see the world, and he died fighting for it. No regrets. Lotta men from the mountains didn't make it home. Like I said, kinda left a shortage of the marrying type. Mama and Daddy needed help here, and then there was Patty. So this is where I stayed."

Then, abruptly, she pushed back her chair and stood up.

"Now, finish up and I'll show you somethin`."

She led us out of the kitchen door and into the back yard.

"Y'know." She said. "We got nearly ten acres here. Used to be more. What with all the neighborhoods and subdivisions happening around here, this here property is worth a pretty penny. This here is the old barn."

She dragged open the side door of an old gambrel-style barn, and walked in. We followed her, and when she flicked a switch, a line of florescent lights came on. Inside were a couple of real old tractors and a whole lot of old horse tack of the working, agricultural variety, hung on racks along the walls. There was old horse-drawn implements, like mowers and plows, and beside the stink of rat shit, the place was rich with the smell of grease and old leather. There was a workbench, rows of old tools, whipsaws and a few real old gas powered implements, and suchlike.

"When Patty and I gone from this world," she said, "someone gonna make a lot of money from all of this."

She glanced up at Lonnie, and with that same fond look, dug him in the gut with her elbow.

"All the scavengers gonna be around, hey Lonnie?"

"Could take it all away for you now Aunt Mildred." He replied.

"Sure you would kid, dang sure you would."

She looked around for moment.

"Place always reminds me of Daddy."

Then she looked back up at us and smiled.

"I won't be sad when I die." She said. " I'll get to see Mama and Daddy again, my brothers, and my old beau. I know he's waitin' on me. I don't guess he will tell me how he died cause there ain't no crying in heaven."

Ralph McLean, a self-proclaimed hillbilly, pictured at home in his kitchen. Known for his humor and plainspoken wisdom, Ralph embodied the easygoing spirit of the Carolina mountains. Surrounded by everyday comforts and the trappings of country life, he carried himself with the pride of a man deeply rooted in his land and heritage.

IT WAS LATE WHEN WE ARRIVED BACK IN HENDERSON-VILLE. Lonnie had passed out in the back seat and was snoring softly. I woke him.

Inside the house, the same tallow-complexioned woman was seated on the same sofa, watching the same television. The same youth sat beside her, with the same child between them. Aunt Jo-lyn was home, and there was excitement in the kitchen because she had brought home a box of books that had been heading for the dump after the passing of an elderly patient at the nursing home. Stan, Miss Patty, and one or two others I did not know were pouring through the contents of the box. They all paused when they saw us, exclaimed with pleasure, and there were hugs and greetings all round.

The books were about quilting and sewing, cooking and home care, a whole bunch of novels, and then an antique, four-volume box-set collection of Winston Churchill's *A History of the English Speaking*

People. Uncle Carl was seated in his usual place, the fourth volume of the series open on his knees. He smiled with his usual sweetness, his blue eyes bright and alert behind a pair of eighties-style, Jeffrey Dahmer spectacles.

The discussion around him was how much the collection was worth. Most of the books were trash, but the four-volume set, which Peter felt pretty sure was a first or second edition, looked like it could be worth a few bucks. Stan was searching on his phone.

"Hell!" He said. "Here on Etsy there is a set just the same for two thousand bucks!"

"Get the fuck outa here!" Exclaimed Miss Patty, and she and Lonnie moved up behind Stan and looked down at his phone.

"Goddamn!" Said Lonnie.

Uncle Carl, meantime, gestured to me to sit down beside him.

"This here." He said. "Is the work of one of the greatest men in history. Winston Churchill! You know him?"

"Sure." I replied. "My daddy once told me that the two men he admired most were Bill Geer, his father-in-law, and Winston Churchill. I'm pretty sure he read those books."

"Well I'll be darned." He said, carefully gathering the book up from his knees, and smoothing down the open pages. He began to read.

"It is not given to us to peer into the mysteries of the future. Still, I avow my hope and faith, sure and inviolate, that in the days to come the English-speaking peoples will, for their own safety and for the good of all, walk together in majesty, in justice and in peace."

The passage was read haltingly, in that beautiful, musical Southern Mountain English of his, and when it was done, he looked up at me, and smiled.

"Ain't that something?"

Rich Man`s War, Poor Man`s Fight

IT WOULD BE APPROPRIATE TO END THIS SMALL EXPLORATION of Southern culture to take a tool at how the Southern man and the military came to be so synonymous. The Depression ended as WWII began, and Southern men flocked to the recruiting offices as the storm clouds broke over Europe. Pretty soon the shacktowns began to empty out as industry and production surged to meet wartime demands, and before long there were just a few shacks left up on Stoney Mountain.

Four children were born under those conditions. Frances did what she did, sometimes, and other times she worked here and there. Old Nick and my daddy never could get along. He was thirteen years old when the two of them got into it for the last time. It's been said about lintheads that they were workers, pushing hard for a better life, and while my daddy lived in that shack, shitting out back, and using mountain laurel to clean his ass, he went to school where he met lintheads, and some blue-bloods maybe, and he figured there was a way out. Nick got his beating, and died not long after, and Daddy walked down that mountain. As I'd heard time and again researching this book; *White trash work hard not to work, work hard to stay right where they are.*

The way my daddy found out was the same as a lot of young men in those days. Donald Williams had several relatives who dropped their tools and signed up for reasons of patriotism, and served through the War. With peace came the G.I. Bill, and suddenly joining up was about more than just fighting. It was about getting an education.

The South has always had a relationship with the military, because the military, in the old days, anyway, was the employer of last resort. If you were too dumb to educate, they'd train you, arm you, and put you in the infantry. If they could educate you, then they would. I guess, because of that relationship, a few words about white trash and the military would be appropriate here.

Dennis E. Pike Sr., Jason's father, pictured in an official U.S. Navy photograph from 1952. He served from 1952 to 1956 and was awarded the Navy and Marine Corps Medal—the highest peacetime military honor—for his bravery at sea. His life and service became a lasting source of inspiration for his son.

This chapter's heading owes its origins to a common practice during the Civil War whereby wealthy men were able to hire draft substitutes to take their places on the front. A figure commonly cited is $300, which was a whole lot of money in the 1860s, and it led to the obvious outcome of poor men manning the battle lines, and getting maimed and killed in wildly disproportionate numbers, in a war very few could barely relate to. The same essential pattern played out during the Vietnam War, with the additional discriminatory tendency of drafting disproportionate numbers of black troops. As Muhammad Ali famously put it, "No Vietcong ever called me nigger."

When I was a kid, I was diagnosed with *osteomyelitis*, thanks to an accidental injury, and besides the pain, I used crutches for a long time, and I lied about it when I joined the army, or they would not have let me in. I was classified as having learning difficulties, and forced to repeat first grade. While I would go on to study at various colleges, and earn two masters degrees, I was advised by my teachers and school counselors to put aside any ambitions to attend college, since it was highly improbable that I would ever qualify. That prognosis was communicated to my parents, and my daddy's response was—"Well son, it'll be coveralls or fatigues for you, you just make your choice."

Ultimately I chose fatigues, but definitely not with a career in the non-commissioned ranks in mind. Through the National Guard, and then the regular Army, I achieved my ambition to study. I earned my degrees, and although I will admit it was often by the skin of my teeth, I was commissioned in the end through the ROTC.

In the 1950s, as high school graduates, both my daddy and Fred Pike enlisted in the Navy, and then Fred went on to train in air traffic control in the Air Force. Both went to college on the basis of the GI Bill, and both emerged into lives and careers that were a million miles away from where they both began. My daddy was raised first as the illegitimate son of a prostitute, and Fred the son of lintheads. Both of them looked at the world around them and figured that there was but one way to get out, and that was the military. A lot of Southern kids thought the same, and that was, as it remains, the basis of that special relationship that the military has with the South.

Dennis Pike with his son, Jason Pike, on the day Jason graduated with a master's degree from Clemson University. For Dennis, who had never imagined his son would reach such heights, the moment was one of pride and astonishment. For Jason, it was proof that the boy who once repeated first grade had persevered, defying expectations to earn a place in higher education.

The South has a long historical association with the military, dating back to the Civil War, and including many, if not most of the overseas conflicts. A majority of military bases are located in the South, and the majority contribution to military manpower derives from the South. The obvious reason for this is that, for many in the South, the military is one of, if not the only pathway out of economic hardship, and in some respects, the employer of last resort. In time, military bases were established across the South, bringing a lot of federal dollars into otherwise impoverished communities. Bases like Fort Bragg in North Carolina, Fort Benning in Georgia, and others throughout the region, brought jobs, infrastructure, and a sense of patriotism and national identity. That made a lot of difference in the post-hookworm era as the lazy class was beginning to stir from their generational lethargy and look around for ways to improve themselves. The military offered the best, and sometimes the only pathway to respectability, training, education, healthcare and upward mobility, and a lot of young men went down that path.

A formal portrait of author Jason Pike during his service as a Lieutenant Colonel in the U.S. Army Medical Service Corps. The uniform, heavy with ribbons and decorations, tells a story of decades of duty and sacrifice. What the photo does not reveal is the long road it took to get here—beginning with a little boy who once failed first grade and struggled to read instructions. From those early setbacks to this moment of achievement, the journey reflects resilience, perseverance, and the refusal to be defined by childhood limits.

The draft was scrapped in 1973, introducing the modern era of an all volunteer army, and that introduced its own disparities. There have been many studies produced over the years that examine the economic incentives that lure the impoverished, and often the unemployable, into the ranks of the military, replacing the old substitute system, and the educational and socio-economic factors of the Vietnam era. In many ways, the net result is somewhat the same. In a region of depressed opportunities, deindustrialization and mechanization, the employer of last resort has traditionally pulled in a lot of disadvantaged youth and minorities, while those that create and prosecute the rules rarely do the fighting, and neither do their sons and daughters. The poor are consigned to the frontline while the rich and educated pass their days in Pentagon cubicles and academies. This is known as the 'economic draft', and while technically the U.S. military is an all volunteer force, economic inequality is still the main force driving recruitment.

As the Duke of Wellington remarked during the Napoleonic Wars: "We have in the service the scum of the earth as common soldiers." In the same way, the military and the impoverished South have always had that obvious compatibility with the rank and file. The military, however, is changing, and becoming more selective as its function is evolving away from the deployment of mass infantry formations to more technically savvy operations that involve educated personnel drawn from the degree-holding class. These days, the opportunities for the unemployable, the scum of the earth, to find employment in the military are diminishing, and it does not seem to me there is a whole lot out there to replace it.

A NOTE TO THE READER

THANK YOU FOR TAKING THE TIME TO READ *BORN OF NOTHING*. We are truly grateful that you chose to spend part of your time with this story and with the lives and histories that shaped it.

The experiences shared in these pages reflect a world that is often overlooked, but that continues to influence families and communities across generations. In telling this story, we drew not only on the history of one family, but also on memories and experiences from our own families who grew up in that same mill-town culture. Our hope is that this book not only sheds light on that history but also encourages reflection on the power of individual choices and the ways in which the past can shape, but does not have to define, the future.

If you found this story meaningful, we would sincerely appreciate your help in sharing it with others. One of the most helpful ways readers can support a book is by leaving a brief review on their preferred retail platform or on Goodreads. Even a short review can help other readers discover the book and decide whether it might resonate with them as well.

For readers interested in learning more about Jason Pike's and Donald Williams' work, additional resources, or speaking engagements, please visit JasonPike.org and IamDonaldWilliams.com.

Thank you again for reading and for being part of this journey.

With appreciation,

Lt. Col. Jason G. Pike, USA, Retired
Donald Williams, Ed.D. / Educator, Research Analyst, Retired

Meet The Authors

Jason Pike / Lt. Col. Jason G. Pike, USA, Retired

LT. COL. JASON G. PIKE, USA, RETIRED, is a decorated combat veteran who served 31 years in the United States Army as both an enlisted soldier and commissioned officer. His career included multiple deployments and 9 years overseas across 5 countries. Throughout his service, he earned more than thirty military awards and badges while completing extensive training and leadership assignments across a wide range of Army units and missions.

Following his retirement from military service, Pike turned his experiences into writing and public speaking focused on resilience, leadership, and life after the military. Drawing from decades of service and personal challenges, he shares practical lessons about perseverance, discipline, and navigating life's difficult transitions.

His first book, *A Soldier Against All Odds*, recounts his journey through the ranks of the Army from age seventeen to retirement, offering a candid look at the realities of military life. His second book, *Out of the Uniform, Back into Civilian Life*, provides practical guidance for veterans navigating the complex process of accessing Veterans Affairs benefits and successfully transitioning to civilian life.

In his third book, *Leading Through the Crossfire*, Pike addresses the challenges of toxic leadership in the workplace and offers strategies for recognizing and overcoming destructive leadership environments. Through his writing and speaking, he continues to encourage others to persevere through adversity and pursue lives of purpose and resilience.

As co-author of *Born of Nothing*, Pike contributes his perspective on perseverance, hardship, and generational change in the American South, adding a voice shaped by decades of military service and leadership.

Donald Williams, Ed.D. / Educator, Research Analyst, Retired

DONALD WILLIAMS, ED.D., was born and raised in York County, South Carolina, in a large family of cotton mill workers. His parents, like generations before them, worked as lintheads. One of more than eighty first cousins and over forty aunts and uncles, he grew up in a close-knit Southern family where love was abundant even when opportunity was limited.

Determined to change the direction of his family's future, Williams became the first in his family to graduate from a major university. He earned three degrees from Clemson University, including a Doctor of Education. Throughout his career, he has taught more than 5,000 students at the secondary, undergraduate, and graduate levels.

Williams served for fourteen years with the Department of Defense Education Activity (DoDEA). During that time, he worked for twelve years as an Education Research Analyst in South Korea, Japan, and the

United States. His work centered on school improvement, leadership development, and the effective use of data to strengthen educational systems.

He believes deeply in the spiritual dimension of life as essential to mental well-being. He views education as a lifelong pursuit, adventure as a source of vitality, and family as the foundation of peace and strength. Today, both of his sons hold doctoral degrees, reflecting the power of faith, education, and intentional choices to change the course of a family's future.

As co-author of *Born of Nothing*, Williams brings both lived experience and scholarly insight to a story of poverty, resilience, and generational transformation.

APPENDIX

Donald and Jason share a joyful moment at a South Carolina mountain overlook. Friends for over 30 years since meeting at Clemson University, their deep passion for exploring family roots shines through—Jason hailing from the rugged backwoods of the North Carolina mountains, and Donald carrying the legacy of linthead heritage.

This photo was taken while Donald was living just south of Camp Humphreys, South Korea Jason came to visit during that time, and the two enjoyed exploring the countryside together.

Here Jason pauses in quiet thought, reflecting on his past and the struggles his family endured to bring him to the place he stands today.

Donald Williams photographed during a recent visit to Alaska. Now retired, he lives in the Appalachian foothills of Georgia, where he enjoys time with family, writing, and serving his community.

Jason Pike with his wife, Beverly, their daughter, and his mother, gathered at a memorial service for his father. The folded American flag in the foreground represents the service and sacrifice of a loved one who had worn the uniform of the United States. More than a symbol, the flag stands as a reminder of duty, legacy, and the cost carried by families across generations. For Jason, the moment tied his own service to the greater story of his family's devotion to country, blending personal grief with enduring pride.

At the Hot Springs with family. From left: Jason Pike, author, with his "shaggy head," his wife Beverly Pike, his brother Dennis Pike, and their father, Dennis Pike, on the far right. At the time, Jason was on active duty in the U.S. Army, assigned as a student pursuing a master's degree. Though he wasn't exactly following military grooming protocol, no one was checking.

A candid moment between Chantel Pike and her father, Jason Pike, following her high school graduation in May 2019 in San Antonio, Texas. Their smiles reflect the deep bond between father and daughter—a relationship shaped by both distance and closeness, by time apart and time reclaimed. For Jason, moments like these are reminders that while service and duty defined much of his life, family remains at the heart of his story.

At the funeral of Fred Pike, Jason Pike (second from left) served as the guest speaker. Surrounded by family and friends, the service became more than a farewell—it was a gathering of stories, shared grief, and enduring kinship. For Jason, speaking that day was both an honor and a duty, a way of giving voice to the legacy Fred left behind while reminding everyone present of the ties that hold a family together even in loss.

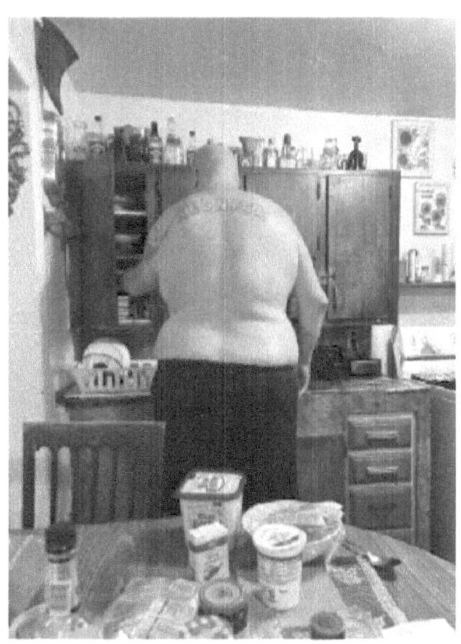

Jeff McLean in his kitchen, the word "Redneck" tattooed boldly across his back. In the Carolina foothills, such a mark carries cultural weight—it is both identity and declaration, reflecting a heritage of working-class pride, resilience, and the unvarnished honesty of rural life.